HIGH IMPACT POWER PRINCIPLES

An Action Guide for Achieving Ultimate Success

PAT COUNCIL

CHARLES THOROUGHBRED SEMINARS
"There's Power In The Present Moment"

VOLUME 1

High Impact Power Principles

An Action Guide for Achieving Ultimate Success

Volume 1
Revised Edition

CHARLES THOROUGHBRED SEMINARS
"There's Power In The Present Moment"

By Pat Council

**Copyright 2001
Pat Council**

All rights reserved. No part of this book may be reproduced in any form except where indicated or except for the inclusion of brief quotations in a review; without permission in writing from the author or publisher

Library of Congress Card Number:

ISBN 0-9716919-0-8

Second printing (revised)

True Thoroughbred Enterprises, Inc.
9930 Chelsea Lake Road
Jacksonville, FL 32256

Printed in the USA

Acknowledgements

There are so many people I have to acknowledge, that if I took the time to list them all, I would probably end up writing another book. I would also probably forget someone, so I would like to thank anyone whose path I've crossed that has either affected me positively or negatively, because all lessons have served to help me discover my true purpose and to better serve mankind.

What's in This Book

You Were Meant to be Here 15

What Fuels Power ………………. …… ………….. 20

Begin At The Beginning 22

Perfection. 25

The Joy of Life **(Have Faith)**. . …... 26

Pain 37

The Joy of Life **(Forgiveness)** 38

Remember When?. 45

Faith And Unconditional Love. 49

The Joy of Life **(The Best Teacher)** 50

Ultimate Dream Sheet 55

Dreams. 57

Effective Goal Setting 58

Creating A Commitment Board. 60

From Ordinary To Extra-Ordinary. 64

Establishing A Plan of Action 66

How To Motivate Yourself........................70

Letting Go Of Negativity........................78

Self-Esteem....................................80

"I AM"...83

Bringing Out The Winner In You..................87

Understanding Cause And Effect..................90

Problem Solving................................95

Daily Quotes...................................101

Visualization..................................104

Self-Talk/Affirmations.........................105

Lighten Up!....................................107

Grateful.......................................113

A Day Of Gratitude.............................114

The Joy of Life **(The Power Behind Purpose)**.......117

Self-Esteem (2)................................128

The Ultimate Joy Of Life **(Love)**................129

It's Okay To Have Self-Esteem..................138

Your Self-Portrait.............................147

Change. 148

Day Of Non-Judgment 149

Physical Fitness 151

Let's Eat 156

Health 159

The Joy Of Life **(Learn To Be)** .160

How To Meditate 162

Happiness At A Glance. 167

What To Do With Your New Information 168

About The Author. 173

"As a man thinketh in his heart, so is he."
Proverbs 23:7

"The greatest possession is self-possession."
Ethel Watts Mumford

Why I Wrote This Book

I believe that anyone who chooses to win can, as long as they do not allow other controllable or insignificant things get in the way or let the negative messages sent by others take root in their head. Following the suggestions in this success guide will help clear a path that will help you achieve your desired successes. We have each been given one life to live and it is important to live it the fullest. Imagine looking back over the years of your life and having nothing to show for it? I am not speaking only of material things; I am speaking of the total package. The total package includes making a value contribution to the society in which you live, building quality relationships, developing more spiritually, emotionally and mentally. Yes, it also means getting the things that you want.

It is important to be able to look at yourself and smile because in your heart, you have done your best and received the best. Instead of wasting time indulging in a lack of self-respect, disrespecting others and just performing as though we have no power and then blaming others for life's situations, we can decide to release our power and excel. The truth is we are all responsible for the outcome of our lives. Even though, we may need help sometimes, it is up to us to reach out and receive help from those who are willing to give it.

It is sad to see people disrespecting the only body they have been given or to see them putting a lid on all their best talents, hopes and dreams by doing the opposite of what it takes to excel. Then there are those who sacrifice their life by constantly trying to run someone else's life or those who live in the past by holding on to something someone did that hurt them. In my seminars, I have met many people with countless excuses for not achieving. Are these bad or lazy people? No, everyone makes mistakes and some do what they know and sometimes what is known is not enough to move life's success needle in their favor. That is why I decided to put this success guide together. We can all use a little help, now and then. Many mentors and teachers helped me put my life on the success track, so I feel obligated to do the same and I feel like I have something to say that could help others. Is my life perfect?

No, but whose life is? I can say that I love the life I am living and I bask in the "joy of life" almost everyday. I also confidently live knowing, that if I do my best, have the right thoughts, take the right actions and use the right tools, life will yield me the kind of results, I desire. So far, so good! There is no perfect life, but the key is to achieve your best life by releasing your personal authentic power such that you make an impact.

The object of the game is to strive for excellence in life. More importantly, you have an obligation to make your life mean something. You have an obligation to keep your heart clean, so you will be able to clearly see those people who need you the most and you will be there for them. It is almost like a "catch 22," you are supposed to be there for yourself and also there for others. That is what *"High Impact Power Principles"* is all about and why it is important to understand what you are capable of as a person. Your doable challenge is to put your life in order so you can tap into your power and excel in the areas that you decide. This book will provide you with some of the guidance you need. As you work your way through this book, you will notice, that a "reading list" has been included. No one person knows everything, so the list has been added so you can tap into the wisdom and knowledge of many experts. It is important that you take it upon yourself to constantly seek character building information. It has been said that "with age comes wisdom", but age does not always bring wisdom. Knowledge, trials, humility, tribulation, spiritual development, and patience bring about wisdom, but even with all the wisdom in the world, we can always learn from others. **My point:** We don't know everything! Use this guide to benefit you, but always continue to seek more information. I wish you all the blessings that come with finding your "joy" in life.

Something to think about: Below is something I encourage you all to take the time to **READ!!!** We are reprinting this information at the permission of Wayne Pickering, a wonderful speaker and friend of mine. Wayne is considered, by many, as "The Ambassador for Health". I believe what Wayne has written paints a perfect picture of the greatness in us all!

Miracles of the Wonderful You

I felt it would be good to share with you the real Wonders of the World and that is YOU!

Of all the living creatures on this planet, not 1 in 10 million are human beings. And you are one. You are a biological rarity and are very important in the eyes of our creator - a RARE GEM! And you are living in the most opportune time in the history of the world! It's our best chance to be mega rich.

In Brooklyn there is a hospital where people wait the rest of their lives waiting for a donor transplant. They actually have to wait for someone to die so they can live. They're called the "POLE PEOPLE" where they walk around all day long carrying a pole of medicine bags with several needles from those bags going into their bodies. To walk around the floor 7 times is their goal and you should see the horrible state of health they're in. It would make your hair cringe. I was watching a program on that 2 nights ago and I had to stop and give thanks for my reasonable state of normalcy. When we get down on ourselves for whatever reason, we can rest assured that there are millions and millions of folks who are a whole lot worse off then we are.

A normal bladder has 10,000 gallons of fluid going through it in a lifetime.

Your ears have 24,500 fibers in each ear just to hear the sound

Your lungs have 600 million air pockets just to take the air into the blood stream.

The outer Layers of the skin are renewed every 2-4 weeks

We have over 60,000 miles of Blood Vessels in the body to keep us working… that's about 2 ½ times around the Globe and pumping enough blood in your entire lifetime to fill a freight train 25 miles long. WOW, That's a boy howdy if I ever heard one.

Your fingernails grow at about the same rate that the Atlantic Ocean is widening.

Did you know that if all the electronic energy in the hydrogen atoms of your body could be used that you could supply all the electrical needs of a large industrialized country for almost an entire week? Talk to me, Baby. Are you there Rick Ernst?

The atoms of your body contain a potential energy of more than 11 million kilowatts per pound…that means that an average person by this estimate is worth more than $85 million dollars. Phooey on that person who told us that we were only worth $1.06 some years back.

And all the atoms of your body sing ... that if you could tune into them, you would hear a perfect harmony.

In so many words, there's more to you than meets the eye and there's no one else like you on the earth or has ever been like you. YOU ARE TRULY UNIQUE!

If all the cell information and the configuration of the components were illustrated in one document, it would take 5 million pages just to print out the complex genetic code of just one single cell. Man oh man. I'm talkin'!

Did you ever consider how perfectly your body is timed and controlled? How it maintains a normal temperature of 98.6 degrees? How the blood pressure is properly regulated and why you breathe an average of 16 times a minute and your heart beats 72 times a minute? How common food is digested chemically and the nutritive part is transformed into body tissue - bone and muscle; blood and skin; hair and nails - and properly distributed while wastes and poisons are eliminated with no ill effect?

You are special with an negotiable self-worth … you're a champ, not a chump... Sure we are experiencing challenging times, but we must go on and continue to try and make a positive difference.

I was reading somewhere about a year ago where a group of Geography students studied the Seven Wonders of the World. At the end of that section, the students were asked to list what they considered to be the Seven Wonders of the World. Though there was some disagreement, the following got the most votes.

1. Egypt's Great Pyramids
2. Taj Mahal
3. Grand Canyon
4. Panama Canal
5. Empire State Building
6. St. Peter's Basilica
7. China's Great Wall

While gathering the votes, the teacher noted that one student, a quiet girl, hadn't turned in her paper yet. So she asked the girl if she was having trouble with her list. The quiet girl replied, "Yes, a little. I couldn't quite make up my mind because there were so many."

The teacher said, "Well, tell us what you have, and maybe we can help." The girl hesitated, then read, "I think the Seven Wonders of the World are:

1. to touch,
2. to taste,
3. to see,
4. to hear,
5. to smell"

She hesitated a little, "and then

6. to laugh
7. and to love."

It is far too easy for us to look at the exploits of man and refer to them as "wonders" while we overlook all what our creator has done, regarding them as merely "ordinary."

May you be reminded today of those things which are truly wondrous … YOU! And all you have to do is "eat good stuff and you'll always be tough."

Wayne "The Mango Man" Pickering = The Ambassador for Health

==

Copyright © 2002 Center for Nutrition, Inc.

==

You are Meant to be Here! Make it Count!

One day after one of my seminars, a young lady came up to me and told me that she enjoyed my seminar, but that the success principles mentioned were not meant for people like her. I will call her, Glenda. The seminar was over and there was a line of people at the table waiting for me to autograph my book. (1st Edition of "High Impact Power Principles".) I did not want to leave Glenda without finding out why she thought the "power principles" I had shared with the room were not for her, so I asked her to wait for me. I quickly autographed my books and then hurried over to Glenda to listen to what she had to say.

She explained that her life had never been easy and that things never worked out for her. She told me, 'she believed it was because she was a mistake'. "Why are you a mistake?" I asked calmly. She went on to share with me that her mother had gotten pregnant by mistake, and her father left her mother and then her mother left her with a relative (her aunt) after she was born. I shared with Glenda that I too, had been abandoned by my mother. She looked surprised. I, then, asked Glenda 'how old she was' and she explained that 'she was 23'. Next, I asked, 'her if she could do anything in her life without having to worry about money what would it be?' She hesitated and then said, 'She would love to start her own business.' She wanted to sell baked goods made from all natural ingredients.

I looked at her and told her that if she was not meant to be here, God would not have given her such a great idea. She became more relaxed and shared that she was always getting ideas about different bake goods of different flavors that she could make. I responded to her by telling her that. 'people who are not meant to be here do not have any purpose, let alone, ideas that come in different flavors and since we all have a purpose, everyone is meant to be here'. My next question was, "What are you going to do with all those great ideas you've been getting?" She said she didn't know. I asked her to invest in a copy of "High Impact Power Principles" and to promise she would complete every exercise. She promised. Almost two years went by then, one day I received an email from Glenda. She had enrolled into college and was learning about business, and she was using the money from the sale of her bake goods to help pay for her studies. They were "a hit", she wrote.

I enjoyed reading Glenda's email, but sometimes I wonder how many other people are not fulfilling their purpose, because they think they were a mistake or because someone convinced them that they were powerless. Take it from me. You were not a mistake, you are not powerless and you do have what it takes to fulfill your purpose. The key is to make the decision to make your life count. Then learn to tap into your **power**, release your **potential**, start serving your **purpose**, and enjoy living a **passionate** life.

Welcome to the beginning of a new and wonderful life. By purchasing this workbook and turning it to this page, you have already started achieving. Because you have decided to take control of and responsibility for your personal success by learning how to tap into your personal power, there will be an automatic shift in the energy in your life. Making the decision to change or improve aspects of your life is part of what it takes to reach your full potential. Taking confident action with clarity is the other part.

You will need a journal or binder with loose leaf paper to write extra notes. Follow each page in this book. Each time you come to a poem let your imagination flow and write, what it means to you. This activity will help you get in touch with your real thoughts and feelings, so have fun with it. Be sure you do not skip any of the daily tasks. Eventually, you will notice personal changes that will take you closer toward living a more satisfying, productive life. Make sure you follow all instructions carefully. Even though it may take you longer than 30 days to complete this workbook, you should notice positive changes before you are near the end of the 30-day mark. Enjoy your journey and especially enjoy meeting the real you! Remember, there is "power in the present moment", so get started, immediately!

Be Powerful,
PAT A. COUNCIL

"The key to everything is patience. You get the chicken by hatching the egg—not by smashing it."
- Ellen Glasgow

"One can never consent to creep when one feels an impulse to soar."
- Helen Keller

It's Time to Get H.I.P.P.

It is time to start a movement, "old school" style. The movement is a surge toward achieving goals and living clean, successful lifestyles. That's right! It is time to get H.I.P.P. (pronounced "hip")! **High Impact Power Principles** is all about designing your life from a position of power and living that way. All the stressing and arguing over the economy is overshadowing the faith of many and some believe that living a dream life is impossible. It has even gotten to the point where people are more preoccupied with the end of the world than they are with living in it and enjoying the world in which we live. We are here now and we are supposing to be living life to the fullest, yet many live in fear.

Understanding our power as human beings will allow us to take more control of our lives and produce positive, productive results. It will become clear that no one or no entity is responsible for providing the things we want most in life. Understanding who we are and what we are made of leads to making decisions that will produce results that will benefit not only ourselves, but our family, friends and others who may need a hand up.

This is what **High Impact Power Principles** is all about. Getting **H.I.P.P.** is about developing a clear understanding of what we are all capable of and then turning on that power to bring out the best in each of us. It is about learning to use the energy you have to bring about the best life that you can command. It is about learning to allow the best to come to you after you have put forth a value-centered effort by using technical and developed knowledge, spiritual principles, and massive faith-filled action. Getting **H.I.P.P.** is about starting where you are today and then improving as each day goes by. It is not about being perfect, but it is about putting for an honest effort, daily. This is a necessary movement we must begin in order to restore a prosperous, positive, productive world filled with people who can make the connection to their God-given power.

It is time to learn to turn unspoken dreams into dreams that are manifested for others to see, so their confidence for achievement and action will begin and continue. Allowing a dream to come forward is all about having the power to subdue negative or unpleasant events that happened in the past or that continues to happen in the present that may be preventing success in relationships, goal achievement, personal happiness, financial increase or in any area that you desire. Now is the time to learn how to plant seeds of hope, so that faith can grow and dreams can be fulfilled.

Learning to accept and understand the power that we were all born with leads to using that power and with the right mental, emotional, and spiritual foundation use of that power will inspire courage in each of us and so many others.

There is no better time for each of us to take control of our destiny than now. Make the commitment to "get H.I.P.P. Let's begin!

POWER IS THE ABILITY TO GET DESIRED RESULTS
DESIRED RESULTS COME FROM THE PROPER USE OF ENERGY.

This is an overview of how to tap into your personal power. These categories will be covered throughout this workbook. Be sure to complete each exercise.

WHAT FUELS POWER?

BEGIN AT THE BEGINNING

Self-assessment - (You will need a mirror large enough to see your entire body and a journal or notebook to write down notes.

Take a good look at yourself, inside and out. After looking carefully at your physical body in the mirror, move in closer and look into your eyes. "The eyes are the windows to the soul." (William Shakespeare) Then, write down some of the changes you want to make that come to mind you Please keep in mind, you are not allowed to "bash" yourself. The purpose of this task is not so you can attack yourself. The purpose is to help you to start paying attention to your life, so be honest with yourself. It is hard to improve in areas that go unnoticed or unacknowledged.

When rose bushes are pruned properly, they grow more beautifully. Look at this as the beginning of your pruning session, so you can produce a more beautiful or handsome and more powerful you.

Besides, it is always good to take a look at yourself every now and then.

In the space below and on the next page, write down information to the following statements:

1. If I could change some thing(s) about myself, I would change:

2. Some things that would make me happy are:

3. Some things that bother me are:

4. I am mostly happy or miserable (pick one).

5. I am happy because:

6. I am miserable because:

7. If I had to describe my body, I would say it is:

Use the space below to write down any other information about yourself. You may write down anything you would like, there are no special rules in this task, except that you be honest and open about you. (Do not ask for anyone else's opinion.)

PERFECTION

Look at me as I stand
From my feet to my hands
I look for perfection through and through
I cannot find it, what am I to do?
As I sit and think with much despondence
I wonder sadly, how can I get beyond this?
For others appeared to be more perfect than me.
I wanted to be more like them, you see.
So the more I tried, I became even sadder.
There was no solution to this heart wrenching matter.
Then one night I fell into a deep sleep
And dreamed a dream I must repeat.
I looked to the sky and saw the answer
The best solution to this "perfection" matter.
The clouds wrote to me across the sky:
Here's the answer you've been seeking by and by.
To find perfection, there is only one way to be
And that my friends, was to be like me.

Write your thoughts below:

The Joy of Life
(Have Faith)

If you want to live a joyful life, you must find inner peace and have faith. One of the ways to bring peace into your life and grow your faith is to learn to control any fears you may have. It seems as though we can always find something to be afraid of, and most of the time it is the thing we fear that keeps us from achieving our goals, wants and needs. Fear has been translated into an acronym, which stands for **F**alse **E**vidence **A**ppearing **R**eal. By allowing false images and ideas to put limitations on how you live, the good things you deserve will always elude you. There are many things that stimulate fear in a person. All of those things are rooted in an individual's belief system established by false teachings and past experiences. It seems as though it is easier to believe in the negative outcome which stimulates fear as opposed to having faith in a positive outcome. Why is that? I have been told that positive thinking is simply living in fantasyland because it is all about denying the problem that exist. If that is the case, then what is negative thinking? In her book, *The Law of Divine Compensation*, Marianne Williamson shares this idea about faith, "Having faith in a positive outcome doesn't mean you're denying a problem or ignoring obstacles; it simply means you're affirming a solution."
Sometimes we are afraid to use our faith, because we want a certain outcome and we think if we believe in a particular outcome and do not get it then, we will have proof that faith is not real and that it does not work. What a lack of faith really means is that there is an absence of the belief in the good things that life can bring. Even if what you are believing in does not happen exactly how you would like it to happen, holding your faith in tact will insure that the best outcome in any situation will present itself. When there is an

absence of faith, fear will set in and with it comes destruction. You will not be able to serve your purpose for being here on this wonderful earth because fear convinces that success is not possible. When you are not able to serve your purpose, you not only hinder and hurt your life, you could be hindering or hurting someone else who needs the benefits of your gift you were meant to share. We are all connected and there are certain aspects of our lives that will thrive based on the actions of others. For example, if all the car mechanics did not follow their purpose, because they lost faith in their abilities and they became singers, dancers or something other than mechanics, if you don't know how to fix a car, what would you do when your car broke down? How would you get to work, church, the grocery store or get to the doctors office that may be too far to walk? We could all make other arrangements, but what would we do when those vehicles broke down? Remember, there are no mechanics, because they all decided to not follow through on their purpose because of fear. Although we are all responsible for the shape our lives are in, no one gets to the top or to the next level, or even to drive to the store up the street, without help from someone else. In this case, it is without the help of the mechanic.

    When I first started selling real estate in 1989, I started in "the red" financially. I had broken up with my fiancée whom I have lived with for five years (I was not spiritually saved then). He had always paid for everything; he even paid for me to go to real estate school. When the break-up happened, I was just starting my career in real estate. I had only sold two houses and had spent the commissions on a down payment for a four door Toyota Camry. Before, I had been driving a Toyota Corolla with only two doors and no air conditioner. Two things had to happen if I was going to become successful at selling real estate in Florida. I needed a four-door car for my customers and I needed to have a working air conditioner. Because I did not anticipate the break-up, I exhausted all of my funds on furniture and a down payment for the new car. I was broke, alone, and yes, afraid. In spite of my fear that I was being put out to live on "nothing", I knew I still had to live. I called my Aunt, who was living in Connecticut and asked for enough money to move and live off of until I could get on my feet. She offered me $1,500.00 and I accepted it. During that time that was not an easy thing for me to do because when I graduated from high school, I left home under unpleasant circumstances. I had a huge chip on my shoulder. In fact, I believe I had the whole tree. Oh what the heck, I had an entire forest on my shoulders! Yes, my life way heavy with drama. I had problems; I left home without even saying good-bye. I left the key on the table and a note saying I wouldn't be back, ever! By the way, there's a lot of truth to the saying "never say never". I have been to see my family countless times since that incident.

    I knew I was going to need more money to sustain myself until I could get my real estate career going. I figured that $5,000.00 would be enough. I applied for a signature loan and I had some credit problems, so the bank turned me down. Within two weeks of being turned down for a loan, I met a real estate broker named George Barnes. He owned his own real estate company. I stopped by his office one day to use the telephone because I was running late for an appointment (cell phones were not as popular then, nor could I afford one). George's assistant was out sick that day, so he was helping his agents manage the office. We talked briefly and I discovered he was a multi-millionaire. I went home and thought about some of the things he and I had talked about. He gave me valuable advice about what it would take for me to become successful and reach my goals. I took some of the information he gave me and I created what I call the 5 "P's": **proper planning, persistence, patience, physical fitness** and a **positive attitude**. I asked him had he ever been afraid that he would not make it. He told me only for a split second. He allowed his f<u>aith</u> to override his <u>fear</u> and he f<u>ocused</u> on his goals and eventually achieved them.

Since the bank had turned me down, I decided to take his advice. I **<u>focused</u>** on my main goal, which was to get $5,000.00 to sustain myself and get my real estate career off the ground. I awakened the next day and decided to ask George to lend me the money or to help me get it. I called and made an appointment to see him. I told him my story, and he told me to go back to the same bank that turned me down, fill out an application, and they would give me a loan this time. I did not ask any questions. I realized that I had met that man for a reason and I trusted that he would not allow me to go back to the same bank and make a fool of myself. Can you imagine if I had allowed my fear to take over? Faith brings tons of possibilities. Fear brings tons of doubt. Instead of allowing doubt to take over, I immediately went back to the bank and filled out an application. The next day the bank called and told me I was approved for the $5,000.00 loan. I went into the bank the same day to sign the paperwork for the newly approved loan. While I was in the bank manager's office, she told me that George had put up a $5,000.00 Certificate of Deposit (CD) as collateral so I could get the money I needed. She said that when they told him about my derogatory credit, he said it did not matter. He told them to give me the money anyway. He was prepared to risk losing his $5,000.00 (CD). You're probably thinking, big deal—what's $5,000.00 to a multi-millionaire, right? Here's what you do not know. George was a multi-millionaire in terms of assets only. At that time, his liquidity had become scarce. He had been very ill and had spent most of his money going to the doctor. On top of that, he had lost a lot of money on other business ventures. During this very same time, he had been considering closing his office to find a new profession (I did not know this when I borrowed the money.). In spite of his situation, he did not allow fear of loss to influence his decision. He listened to his heart.

It all worked out in the end like a blockbuster movie. I paid the money back and became the top agent in my company within six months. During those six months I read every book about sales that I could get my hands on. One day, I stopped by to see George and I told him he needed a better-looking sign for his office. He told me that he was losing interest in his business. I felt obligated to do something, but I did not know what. He said if someone came along and wanted the company, he would give it away. I opened my mouth and out came the words "Don't give it away, I will come in and run it for you!" I had never run a business before, but after hearing myself say I would run his company, I knew in my heart that I could do it. I was a fast learner.

I became the office manager at George Barnes Realty. I re-organized, created new policies to motivate the existing agents. Some agents that had left returned and some that were not interested in producing, left, because I was full of energy and looking for movers and shakers, not loungers and layers. We changed the sign on the building, changed the colors to attract more customers and to let the existing clientele know that George Barnes was back and better than ever! Revenues increased within the first year and continued to go up every year after that. George Barnes Realty regained and eventually passed its original position in the real estate market. Can you imagine how different things would have been if George had allowed fear to alter his decision to put up his own money, so I could get a loan? He did not and he received far more than $5,000.00. He could have considered that because I was an agent working for another company, I could have used the money he helped me get my business going to take over his market, yet he still gave me the money. I, in turn, acted out of loyalty because of his fearless action and my fearless response, we both prospered. I eventually left the company because I believed my purpose had been served and I wanted to go in a different direction. We had both served each other well, without fear. Our fearless actions allowed divine order to run its course. I left in 1995 and as of the time that I am now revising this book (2013), he is still flourishing in business in the same office and I am happily living my purpose. So if you are letting fear stop you, remember, you only have one life to live. Let your faith come forward and take a chance on yourself or someone that you know needs help. When you live in fear, you place limitations on your entire life, which can affect those closes to you. In order to successfully complete this book, it is important to face any fears that may be stopping you from living your dream life. If you have a problem with fear, there are ways to eliminate or control your fears. A few suggestions are listed below:

1. Expose myths that cause fear. Many believe that if a Friday falls on the 13th of the month, things are going to go wrong or bad things will happen. It is just another day, if things go wrong on every Friday the 13th; it is only because of your expectations. What other negative myths or beliefs have you been holding on to that could be keeping your fears alive; thereby preventing you from attracting good things into your life? Take the time to educate yourself about the things you fear the most and you will find the strength to overcome your fear.

2. Learn to trust someone. Stop saying you do not trust people! There are lots of trustworthy people in this world. Find someone you can trust and share what you are feeling. Be careful not to choose someone who will cater to your fears. Ask whomever you choose to be truthful with you and tell you all the reasons why your fears are holding you back. If this is too difficult, express your fears in your journal.

3. Practice thinking positive. If you examine your fears closely, you will find that they all possess negative undertones. Practice thinking positive thoughts or look for something funny and positive about your fears. Overtime, your fears will begin to minimize, because you will be looking at the lighter side of life.

4. Increase your spirituality. The more spiritual you become, the smaller your fears will become or the more control you will have over your fears. Spirituality will give you a sense of peace, a better understanding of the role you should be playing in life, the courage to face and conquer your fears, and you will discover how irrational your fears are, because your courage will begin take over.

One unconquered fear can stop you from living your life to the fullest. Take the time to identify what has been holding you back and make the commitment to take control of it today, because there is "power in the present moment."

As you do the next exercise and identify any fears that may exist in your life, take a moment and reflect on how the fear has brought limitations into your life. If you feel you need therapy to get beyond your fears, do not hesitate to seek help.

Release Your Fears Exercise

In this exercise, you will have the opportunity to do some soul searching. Before you can move forward, receive good things or have the kind of life you desire you must find your feelings of gratitude, love, and peace. The best way to do this is to become aware and acknowledge any fears that may be holding you back from releasing your personal power.

Take a moment to imagine what a life without fear would be like. Of course, the main objective is to learn to manage your fears, so that you will always continue to move forward.

You may need a few sheets of paper or write your answers in your daily journal if you need more space. Please do not rush through this exercise. Proper completion of the exercise will help you get in touch with the real you and then you will be able to take the appropriate action for your success.

1. Make a list of your fear(s).

2. Write down why you feel afraid and where you think this fear comes from.

3. How have your fear(s) held you back?

4. Can you determine why your fear(s) is/are irrational? Write the reasons down. If you cannot figure out why your fear(s) is/are irrational, ask someone you trust (they must have a positive attitude, be logical and honest). Seek out a therapist, or talk to your spiritual advisor (If you don't have a spiritual advisor, consider getting one).

5. What changes would you like to make?

6. What changes are you committed to making?

7. Who will you ask to help you eliminate or get your fear(s) under control?

8. What help do you think is needed?

9. When are you going to begin?

PAIN

If you happen to have someone,
who's a thorn in your side.
Maybe he was sent by God,
to be your mortal guide.
When you seem to despise
those ugly things he can do.
Look a little closer,
those ugly things are in you.
So make the change and understand,
that you will only gain.
A better life will come your way,
And eliminate all your pain

Write down your thoughts about this poem:

The Joy of Life
(Forgiveness)

As a child, if you did something that was considered to be wrong you were punished? You made mistakes and in some cases you were chastised, but always forgiven. After being forgiven, most of us, as children would run out to play and forget the whole incident. In other words, you resumed your life as if nothing happened. You forgave and you were forgiven and life progressed.

How about if you had a fight with your friends in grade school? In time, you would forget what the fight was about and go back to being friends and having fun. Why is it when we become adults we lose that way of thinking? We lose the innocence that allows us to forgive ourselves and others. As an adult, mistakes still happen, and once some type of corrective action has been taken (by the law or in some other smaller way), we refuse to let go of the incident. It does not matter if we made the mistake against ourselves, or if someone else did something to hurt us. We find it difficult to forgive others or ourselves. We keep holding ourselves accountable for a past we can not change, whether we have done something to correct it or not. We not only refuse to forgive, we keep the problem alive by sharing it with others, as though they can use some magic and change the past. The truth is we want the whole world to know that we have been hurt emotionally and we want their sympathy or for them to fix our lives. Another reason is that we sometimes want others to share in the guilt feelings we have. We also share what someone has done to us because we want to justify what we are doing to them, such as no longer speaking to them or worse. I have a good friend who had some children out of wedlock. When these children were conceived, my friend was ignorant to the laws of God. He chose to become a Christian and is faithful to his religion and he nurtures his spirituality. After changing his life he tried to make amends by being a better father to his children; however, the mothers involved, except for one, would not allow him to see his children, because of how had treated the mothers in the past. He has asked their forgiveness and yet their anger and unforgiving attitudes would not allow them to forgive him. Their unforgiving spirit made them all blind to the fact that they were hurting their own children by using them as weapons against their father. Not only that, the children who were born with the innocence God gave them, were being taught to not only hate others, they were learning not to like themselves. When non-forgiveness is practiced, many innocent bystanders are caught in the crossfire of hate and animosity. There are no acts of vengeance you can inflict on another without hurting yourself and possibly others. The "you reap what you sow" concept is always in effect and it is not something we can control.

The concept behind forgiving is to let go of something so you can move forward with your life. Rest assured, no good deed goes without rewards and no bad deed goes unpunished, but the type of punishment is not always up to us, so let it go.

Clean your emotional, mental, and spiritual slate and get on with your life! In fact, make the decision to live a renewed and better life. Life is supposed to be lived so you can reach a point of fulfillment and personal power and so you can learn to use your talents to empower someone else. In one form or another, that is all our purposes. Whether you are a doctor, nurse, lawyer, realtor, cab driver, bus driver, teacher, accountant, etc., you have been put here to serve, and not to criticize, constantly condemn or judge others. That kind of energy will prevent you from living your best life. Your power to attract what you want will slow down and sometimes come to a halt. **(See the chart on page 131.)** When you criticize others, you create unnecessary inner turmoil, which takes away your joy and holds you back in life. Most people make mistakes because at the time, they think they are doing the right thing or because they simply were not taught the right way to handle life's situations. That is not your problem or your fault, is it? However, it may be your purpose to educate or correct someone so you can make their life better, or maybe even take away their pain and confusion. What's in this for you? You will find the answers to "peace, prosperity, and positive attraction" as you continue to help others. When we are unable to forgive, we stay in a constant state of judgment, criticism, and condemnation. In that state, you can not help anyone, including yourself. That type of energy takes its toll on your health and your overall lifestyle. Carrying around unresolved issues only increases the pain you feel. Releasing your judgment of others; making the conscious decision to help and serve, instead of criticizing or holding a grudge, will take away your own sorrow and pain. Practicing forgiveness when needed is one of the ways to bring joy into your life. You feel more in control of your life and your destiny when you're able to let go of animosity toward others. Your prosperous future will become clearer.

It is easy not to forgive, to always criticize, and knock someone down. To enjoy your own life, you must release your attachment to the negative in order to attract the positive. Do you sometimes wonder why bad things always happen to you? The "Law of Attraction" says you are doing it to yourself. The dark cloud that follows you may be generated by your own thoughts and feelings. To carry unforgiving feelings means to carry hatred and anger in your heart, constantly. Joy and hate cannot easily co-exist because they are both felt internally. This is what produces inner turmoil and unnecessary burdens. Learn to laugh, love, release the past, visualize your future, and live in the present. You owe yourself the gift of joy, especially if you have children in your household! Your misery and pain will hurt them. Remember, children learn what they live. To identify something that may be stopping your joy, complete the tasks on the next page.

Follow these instructions:
Take a minute to make a commitment to yourself.
Repeat the next phrase aloud: *"I will complete the tasks in this workbook. I will continue working. I am ready to practice forgiveness, so I can live a happier life and make a valuable contribution to the society, I live in and so I can have a happier environment."*

Forgive and Forget Exercise

As it was stated earlier, you cannot attract anything good unless you have a loving heart.

Exercise: Take your time when answering the questions in this task. Once again, you must be very honest with yourself. Do this exercise in an environment that makes you comfortable. You may consider being alone so you can be more open with yourself. If you feel the need to cry or scream, do so. The objective is to release the negative, so the positive can shine through.

Power Tip: Remember, you are not dwelling in the past by completing this exercise. Your problem exists because you have not allowed yourself to forgive, so you are actually dealing with the present.

1. Who are you angry with that you haven't forgiven?
   (List as many names as you would like.)

2. Why are you still angry with them?

3. Has your being angry with them negatively affected your life? (Before you answer No, remember you are looking to receive the desires of your heart. If you are not receiving what you desire, then you are being affected.) If yes, explain how.

4. What would make you feel better?

5. What would you like the one with whom you are angry to do for you?

6. Is it possible that you are unwilling to forgive someone who, due to his or her own environment or up bringing, may not be capable of giving what you are asking for?

7. What are your flaws?

8. Have you ever done anything to disappoint or hurt someone else? If yes, would you like to be forgiven?

9. Is it possible that you are angry with yourself and have not been able to forgive yourself because you made a mistake, yet you are blaming someone who may have been involved?

Extra Power Tip: Remember, it is possible to harbor feelings of unforgiveness toward someone else because you are unable to forgive yourself for making a mistake. Sometimes we blame others for the bad choices we made. If that is the case with you, accept responsibility for your actions. You are human. You simply made a mistake. Now let go and live. Be sure to write your feelings in your journal.

REMEMBER WHEN?

This exercise is designed to help you become more self-aware and to help you explore some past experiences that you may have never dealt with. Recognizing any problems or unresolved issues can allow you to clean areas of your life that may be clouding your judgement and preventing you from enjoying life or achieving your goals.

Why Remember? It is time for you to clean your mental and emotional closet. This task is about moving forward, not staying in the same place mentally, emotionally, or spiritually. It is very important that you spend some time away from everyone to effectively complete this exercise. Write down some of the experiences you have had that hurt you the most or that have had an extremely negative effect on you. Write down whatever you feel is important to you. If you have more than one experience, feel free to make copies of this page or write in your journal.

For example: Are you still carrying the pain from a past relationship? Were you abandoned by someone you trusted and loved? Did you have an unpleasant experience that you have not been able to bring closure to in your mind? Write any experience down, no matter what it is. This exercise is to be completed by you, alone.

Write your experience down now:

Possible Solutions:

1. What would it take to make you feel good again?

2. Is it possible for you to share your feelings with the individual that may have caused you pain?

3. Do you have the courage to share your feelings with the one who caused you pain?

4. Write a letter to the individual who hurt you or a letter describing your feelings about the experience you have had.

5. Once you have written your feelings down in a letter, if your experience involves an individual, pretend you are that person and write what you wish they had said to you. (Even if the individual(s) is/are deceased, still write their response.) The objective is to release what you have been hanging onto for too long and get the closure you need.

6. List other solutions you feel would make you feel better. If you feel you need therapy, write that down and take action.

Power Tip: Remember, if you choose to confront someone do not confront him or her with the expectation that they are going to embrace you with kindness and understanding.

They may display harsh resentment toward you for even mentioning the old incident. Do not waste time trying to change the attitude of the person who offended you. The only objective is to have the opportunity to tell them how you feel. You are not responsible for another person's behavior. If they will at least listen, say what you have to say and leave. If they won't listen, leave, knowing that you had the courage to confront them and let it go. *Write down* your act of confidence and courage, and feel good about that. You may want to tear up the sheet you wrote your unpleasant experience on. This may be a good way to let go and move on. Keep it, only if reading it will make you feel better, but please keep in mind the objective is to let go and move on.

Faith and Unconditional Love

If you want to forgive, replace an unforgiving heart with one filled with unconditional love. If you allow yourself to feel love, you will not only forgive, you will develop the power to control your destiny and become more successful than you ever imagined. If revenge is what you have been seeking, becoming a success is sometimes the best way to get it. Learn to love all people, including, yourself. Learn to love what you do, and the life you have right now and before you know it, you will begin to receive all the things you desire.

If you want to eliminate fear, replace it with faith and love. Real faith will give you the courage and strength to achieve whatever goal you set out to achieve. Love will cause you to keep going, even when you want to stop and it will keep you focused only on what will bring you the best for your life.

An affirmation to repeat:
I release all anger and unforgiving feelings and replace them with unconditional love. I have strong feelings of faith, so I believe God will give me strength to conquer anything. I am better than ever and good things come to me now!

Power Tip: Repeating the above affirmation will help you feel more confident and happy as you embark on your journey of success filled with power.

The Joy of Life
(The Best Teachers)

There are many kinds of teachers in life "the tyrant" and "the healer" (as I have decided to name them) plays an important role in your mental, emotional, and spiritual growth.

Has there ever been someone in your life that seemed to have turned your emotions upside down and you wanted to walk away, but you felt as though you couldn't? Then one day you woke up and decided that enough was enough! All of a sudden you had the courage and emotional stamina to tell the tyrant in your life to go away and once he or she was gone, you not only felt relieved, you felt more confident, and ready to face anything. If none of the above has happened to you, read on because if it does happen you will be ahead of the game. Although we often refer to those situations as burdens being lifted, they are more than that. These situations occur, because they are lessons of growth designed to lead you toward living a powerful and successful life. If you encounter the tyrant it is because you were stubborn, and refused to listen to any warnings or wise advice from someone close to you or even a stranger you may have briefly encountered, or you failed to seize the opportunity to learn the lesson, the easy way. Another reason those heart wrenching situations may occur is because, you may be over looking or ignoring your purpose and when God has a plan for you, he does expect you to carry it out. A third reason might be that you are simply being tested. Life holds great rewards for us all but the rewards are not always equal, so some of us have to endure extra tests of humility, obedience, faith, and patience. We must be tested to make sure we can handle the responsibilities that come with receiving greater rewards. Also, consider the **"law of attraction," "law of retribution"** and the **"law of detachment"** as possible reasons for the tyrant or tyrants in your life (Yes there can be more than one tyrant and healer):

The **"law of attraction"** implies that you are simply attracting what you are. If you are attracting things you do not want, that could mean there is something undesirable in you. The tyrant or unpleasant situation could be your mirror. Once you eliminate your undesirable quality (qualities), the tyrant or unpleasant situation will go away and you will begin to attract your hearts desires.

The **"law of retribution"** implies that you have done something that is considered to be a Universal wrong. In the Universe, "no bad deed goes unpunished and no good deed goes without being rewarded", so the tyrant may be a part of the punishment designed to teach you a lesson. When you wrong others, once again life becomes your mirror and someone comes along who wrongs you and the situation keeps happening to you, or the tyrant remains in your life until you learn your lesson. If you don't learn the lesson, more tyrants appear.

The **"law of detachment"** should come into play when it is time for you to let go of something or someone you may not want to let go. As long as you remain attached to what you should let go of, you are interfering with receiving your greater good and altering your life's journey. By not moving forward to the next level you could be delaying someone else's good, as well and once that takes place, the "law of retribution" and/or the "law of attraction" is activated and the aggravating tyrants show up again. For example, someone who may have seemed perfect for you when he or she came into your life, may all of a sudden become someone who causes you a lot of emotional pain or strife and you constantly ask yourself why is that person in your life. They are in your life for a reason and when your situation is said and done, you should be able to look back and see what you might have been able to see sooner had you not been so attached to the situation.

Because, some things require a learning period in life the easiest way to move forward and reap your rewards is to learn by using "the healer." I call that life's teacher, "the healer," because he or she will listen as you share your thoughts and feelings. They will also keep what you share confidential and they will share information that will guide you toward a more rewarding destiny. Please do not assume that "the healer" is a psychiatrist or a psychologist. He may or may not be one. The healer is someone who will allow you to share and as you share, you will have revelations to share that will cause you to "heal" emotionally and increase your spirituality. The objective is to grow spiritually and emotionally, so that you will be able to go to the next level in life, receive your rewards and the desires of your heart; you will also become strong enough to handle any obstacle that may confront you. Keep in mind, that the healer is not someone who agrees with all your ideas and opinions. We grow when someone cares enough to correct us and help us get on the right path. For example, one of my healers was a Pastor named Elwyn Jenkins. During that time my heart was filled with anger and I did not trust anyone because of things that had occurred in my life during earlier years. I met Pastor Jenkins before the tyrant entered into my life. Divine intervention came because God knew I would need someone to guide me toward spiritual stability, listen to me share my thoughts, and to position me to be "healed." Once the tyrant showed up I went on the emotional ride of my life and that ride lasted almost four years. The law of attraction was in full effect and because I knew nothing about the law of detachment, I hung onto my misery for dear life. The more the tyrant attacked me, the more I shared to the healer. Finally, one day I woke up and realized that my mental defenses that had been weak, had become stronger and my spiritual and emotional stamina had become powerful. I was able to let the tyrant go. The tyrant did go and I received great rewards. I learned to look to God for my supply and not to someone who wanted to manipulate me for their purpose. I learned that if I trusted others, most of them would become trustworthy. If I met someone who was not trustworthy, I learned not to take it personal and they usually disappeared from my life without chaos. I learned to love me and that it was "okay" to make a mistake. I learned the fine art of forgiveness, kindness, and humility. I learned to accept and expect good things in my life. I learned to complain less and to become solution oriented. I opened my heart, loved others, and received love in return. I discovered my purpose and gladly took action. I learned to accept responsibility for the role I played in my own unhappiness. I learned to be happy. I learned the joy of life. I learned so much during those four tumultuous years, yet I did not realize how much I was learning. I was learning from the tyrant who I allowed to keep me in a state of misery and from the healer who listened and only spoke with wisdom when necessary. They both guided me toward my purpose and a better life.

    We do not always have to like what's happening to us, but we should try to understand the lessons we are supposed to learn or the discoveries we are supposed to make. We should also remember that where there is a tyrant, there is also a healer. Also, where there is a tyrant there is a lesson to be learned and if you can not figure it out, the healer will be there to guide you. Become strong enough to release the tyrant and wise enough to recognize and accept the healer. Remember, you only have one life, open your heart, receive your reward, and live!

The Ultimate Dreams Sheet

Be honest and open with yourself during this exercise!

"You have not, because you ask not."

When was the last time you dreamed about the things you wanted for your life? It's not about whether you think you can get what you want, it is about allowing yourself to dream and feel the lifestyle you want. Keep in mind that lifestyle is not just about things. Lifestyle includes the type of relationships you want to have and the overall atmosphere you want to have as apart of your life. Lifestyle includes your life's passion. What do you want to <u>really</u> do for a living?

Write down everything you have ever wanted to have and everything you now desire. Write down all the things you have ever wanted to try. When writing down your dreams, do not hold back. Feel free to write all over the pages and draw pictures, if necessary. Feel free to write down anything you have ever dreamed of having, becoming or doing. Remember, these are your dreams. This is the new vision for your life. Do not worry about how you will get what you want, just dream and write. Get started!

(Blank Page) **Continue dreaming…**

DREAMS

When you're sitting all alone and
You don't know what to do,
Dream a wonderful dream, it
Just might come true.
Think of your prince charming
Never be afraid
Visualize a castle or a pool, in
Which to wade.
See a winning wonder in
Everything you do.
Dream a wonderful dream, it
Just might come true.

Write your thoughts after reading this poem:

Effective Goal Setting

Committing to your goals in writing greatly improves your chances of actually following through on the promises you have made to yourself. This task should be completed in one day. Remember; do not skip any exercises unless instructed to do so.

Exercise: Write your goals in each category. There will be some goals you want to achieve immediately; therefore, you should identify your goals as short term or long term. Feel free to borrow some of your goals from your dream sheet.

Power Tip: Short-term goals are goals to be achieved within 30, 60, 90 days, 6 months and 1 year. Long-term goals include those that exceed one year. Take the time to complete goals for each time period. Also remember, your goals must match your self-image. You will not make a million dollars until you think like a million-dollar person. To raise your self-image and bring more order to your life, use the plan concept outlined in my book, P.O.W.E.R.. Raise your level of expectation for yourself, by going outside of your comfort zone. Start visiting the kinds of places that match the lifestyle you want to live. For example: It doesn't cost to go and sit in the lobby of an expensive hotel or ask for a pricelist and to be shown one of their suites. It also doesn't cost to try on a few expensive outfits or to simply look and price things.

A Guide For Establishing Goals

1. **Spiritual** – Find a church where you can fellowship and worship. Set a daily time to pray, read the Bible, and meditate.

2. **Education** – Commit to learning something new and learning more about your profession. List the kind of degree you would like to have or skills you want to learn.

3. **Financial** – Create a savings plan, a retirement plan and seek information for improving your financial position. Talk to a financial counselor, if necessary. Take investment classes, online or in a classroom setting.

4. **Social/Entertainment** – Write down the kind of vacation you would like to take and some of the social events you would like to attend. What will you do for fun periodically?

5. **Family** – Write the desires you have for improving your relationship with your family and friends. If you wish to be married write down the kind of spouse you are looking for. If you need to repair a relationship with a family member write the name down.

6. **Health/Physical** – Map out a plan to improve your health by eating right and exercising. How much would you like to weigh? Get help from a professional if you need to.

7. **Income** – How much money would you like to earn? How much money do you need to get the things you want? Write your income based on the amount you want to earn in 30, 60, 90 days, and 1 year. Your income

should match the amount of money needed to get the things you want.

8. **<u>Professional</u>** – List the type of profession you would like to pursue, if you are not already in that profession.

9. **<u>Personality</u>** – Put in writing what you would like your personality to be like and how you would like to be perceived by others. How do you want people to remember you?

Your Ultimate Goal Sheet

1. **Spiritual** –

2. **Education** –

3. **Financial** –

4. **Social/Entertainment** –

5. **Family** –

6. **Health/Physical** –

7. **Income** –

8. **Professional** –

9. **Personality** –

(Feel free to use as many sheets as necessary.)

Creating A Commitment Board

Purpose: I am labeling the vision board as a commitment board. Only put photos of things you are committed to working to achieve. The commitment board will serve as your visual aid. Once it has been completed, the board is to be placed where you can see it at least once everyday. Seeing pictures of your goals will make the possibility of achieving them seem more real to you and enhance your desire to work toward realizing them.

Instructions for creating your board: Once you have finished your dream sheet, find several magazines and look through them for pictures that match your goals and dreams. As you find the pictures that match your goals and dreams, cut them out and paste them to a cardboard. The board should be large enough, so you can fit pictures of all your desires on it. Find as many pictures as you can.

If you cannot complete your board within one day, simply continue working until you are done. This will be a board you will be keeping around for a while, so move on to the next exercise, but be sure to complete the board as soon as possible.

Power Tip: Make sure you look at your wish board every day. Ask yourself; did you do anything to bring you closer to achieving your goals? At the top of your board, you may want to write thought provoking statements or questions that will make you conscience of your goals, such as: **"Hello (Your Name), did you do anything to take you closer to your goals today? If not, get back to work! Go Now!"** Make sure you read the above statement out loud everyday, if you choose to write it on your board as a reminder. Please feel free to create your own inspirational statement. Whatever you have to write to keep you on track, do it. Remember, in order for you to manifest the things on your board, you must be in alignment with them. In other words, you must have faith that you can have the things you desire and believe that if you do the work, opportunities will present themselves that will allow you to achieve every goal you set. Simply pasting pictures on a board will not be enough.

From Ordinary to Extra-ordinary

When I moved to Jacksonville in 1989, I made friends with a young lady. We were both in our 20's when we met and we immediately became friends and off to the Disco clubs we went. We would hang out at my apartment on the weekends and have fun. Eventually, my goals changed and other events occurred that caused us to go our separate ways. We reconnected just in time for her to come to my very first seminar. That night I taught about goal setting, developing a plan of action, and other success tips. Because she was my friend, it never dawned on me that she would even consider using the information I taught that night. (Sometimes your friends and family know you too well to take you seriously.) Especially since, she knew me when I did not have any serious goals. A few weeks later, she and I talked. I listened with much surprise as she shared her goals and told me about all the changes she wanted to make in her life. She had mapped out her goals and a plan of action. Today, she has a new car, a new house, new husband and her own business. She achieved several of her goals because she took the time to map out a plan of action. Now, she is planning to achieve bigger and better things. Realizing that with a good plan, she could achieve almost anything, she is continuing to expand her sphere of influence and working to achieve more, while improving her overall lifestyle. She is taking her life to the next level.

Get the picture! An action plan is an extension of your goals. They should be more specific and written out, so that you have a clear vision of what steps you should follow to reach your goals. Your action plan should have projected deadline dates. Don't stress over a deadline date, it is just a projection, but it will serve as excellent tracking for your journey. You will also discover how serious you are about achieving the goals that you set for your life. Write out a plan of action for every goal you have. I suggest you keep copies of your goal page and plan of action pages together in a separate folder, and your notebook, so you will have more than one copy. Keep a copy with you when possible and read them whenever you can.

Power Tip: If you do not have a clear vision once you have written out your plan, try again or ask for help. You can get some answers to your questions by joining one of our forums. Visit: forum.designingyourlifetoday.com. You must be able to see your beginning clearly. The rest of your path will reveal itself as you move forward with confidence. Goals without a plan are called a dream. To help you write out your plan more clearly, take some advice from Stephen Covey, the author of "The 7 Habits of Highly Effective People," "Begin with the end in mind." (For a copy of "The 7 Habits of Highly Effective People." Visit: Designingyourlifetoday.com.)

Establishing a Plan of Action

Once you have had some fun with your ultimate dreams sheet and committed to your goals in writing, take the time to create a plan or road map for realizing your goals. Most people fail to realize their goals, because they never take the time to create a plan of action. Taking the time to write out how you intend to achieve your goals means you are more committed than ever. It will also reveal the tools that you may need in order to complete the goals that you set.

Look at it like this; if you needed to drive to Arizona and you did not know how to get there, it would be smart to buy a map that showed the directions to Arizona. Then, you would map out the route that would take you to Arizona with the least amount of problems. A plan of action for achieving your goals should be done the same way. Using the example below, map out your plan on the page we have provided. The example on the next page was taken from a plan I used for myself during my time in real estate. As you will see, a plan of action does not have to be long. It only has to be a clear road map to a certain goal destination. No matter what your interests are a plan will take you closer to the achievement of your goals and the realization of your dreams.

Writing out a plan of action isn't anything new. This process of achievement has been around since biblical times. "Write the vision and make it plain…." Habakkuk 2:2

An example of a non-business plan of action has been included, for use in everyday life. We all have a goal that we want to achieve whether we are in business or not, but to effectively achieve it, you must have a plan.

EXAMPLES

Action Plan I (Business)

Today's Date: April 24, 1997

1. **Goal to be achieved**   **Date to achieve by**:
   Increase my income by $5,000   7/24/97 – 90 days

2. **Plan of Action:**   **Start Date:**
   1. Make 3 more sales a month   4/24/97
   2. Give out 5 more business cards a day   4/24/97
   3. Do follow-up calls everyday   5/01/97
   4. Contact all past clients   5/02/97
   5. Send follow-up letters to past clients   5/09/97

3. **What I Need to Achieve My Plan:**

   a. Tools—Extra business cards, Criss Cross Directory, Tracking Sheets

   b. Knowledge—How to write effective sales letters

   c. Extra help needed—A Personal Assistant

Action Plan II (Personal)

Today's Date: April 24, 1997

1. **Goal to be achieved:**   **Date to be achieved by:**
   Save $500.00 or more in an account   8/24/97 - 120 days

2. **Plan of Action:**   **Start Date:**
   1. Determine current financial situation   4/24/97
   2. Write out a budget (include bills, necessities
      clothes, fun items, wants)   4/24/97
   3. Keep an expenditure diary for 2 weeks   4/25/97
   4. Determine what expenditures to eliminate   5/09/97
   5. Find a way to save no less than $42.00/week   5/10/97

3. What I need to achieve my Plan:
   a. A job or income of at least $30,000 or more per year

   b. Discipline

   c. A promotion on the job

PLAN OF ACTION

Today's Date:

1. <u>**Goal to be achieved**</u>   <u>**Date to achieve by:**</u>

2. <u>**Plan to Achieve**</u>   <u>**Start Date**</u>

   a.

   b.

   c.

   d.

   e.

4. <u>**What I need to achieve my plan:**</u>

   a. Tools –

   b. Knowledge needed –

   c. Extra help needed-

(Make copies if needed)

HOW TO MOTIVATE YOURSELF

Regardless of what your field of endeavor is, staying motivated is very important. Although you may have developed well thought out goals and your plan of action is all set to go, your ability to stay motivated is what will give you the energy you need to continue toward achieving set goals. In addition to keeping you energized, staying motivated will enhance your ability to stay focused, improve creativity and increase your desire to see your goals realized. While staying motivated is important, it is not always an easy task. Some of the tips listed below will help you:

1. **<u>Always Use Positive Language</u>** –When a problem arises, do not make it worst by using negative phrases. Recognize all problems as an opportunity to learn a better way for doing things. Make it a habit of immediately replacing any negative phrases you might use with positive ones, so you can see a better outcome.

2. **<u>Read Positive Phrases</u>** –Start and end each day by reading something positive. "It Only Takes One Minute to Change Your Life" by Willie Jolley makes excellent reading, especially if you don't have a lot of time. Read some of your favorite verses from the Bible (If you don't read the Bible, Proverbs is a great place to start). Also, you may refer to the reading list included in this workbook.

3. **<u>Visualize Positive Results</u>** –Try imagining yourself as though you have already achieved your goals and are enjoying the fruits of your labor. No matter what your life is like, today, see yourself living a life that is perfect for you. That will give you something to look

forward to and inspire you to continue until you achieve your dream. Do not be afraid to spend some time dreaming big dreams, but be sure you are taking measurable action. For example: Imagine yourself in a large house, new car, the perfect relationship, lots of friends, and money or riding to your favorite restaurant in a limousine. See your chauffer opening the door and you are getting out in your favorite outfit. Do not be afraid to imagine opulence. Remember, you are currently imagining something that isn't your reality, but it can be. Once you return to reality, you may feel a little inadequate. That is the beginning of some of the feelings you need to get going, so take action immediately. Refine your plan and get to work! Remember: do not be afraid to dream! The dreams are yours, so you have the right to dream anything you want.

4. **Do Something to help someone else** – Nothing can motivate you better than the joy you feel after you have done something to help someone who really needs you. Especially, if what you are doing falls in line with your life's purpose. A part of our reason for being is so we can help each other or give of ourselves when it is most needed. Constantly taking or expecting others to give to you can be a real downer when things do not go the way you expected. Take the time out to give of yourself and much more than you expected will find its way to you, automatically.

5. **Dress Up** – Think back to when you were a kid. Remember how good you felt when you wore a new pair of shoes, a new dress, or new slacks to school? Well, nothing has changed. No matter how old you are,

putting on your favorite outfit or purchasing something new will make you feel like you're ready to charge forward to success. Be careful not to purchase beyond your spending power. You do not have to buy something expensive, just the newest of the item will be rejuvenating.

6. **Spend Time Around Positive People** - When you feel your motivation slipping away, one of the best ways to put it back intact is to call your mentor, business coach or life coach. If you do not have one, you should take the necessary steps to find one; however, until you find a mentor, seek out people who have a positive attitude and are living their life on purpose. Even if you have a mentor or coach, you want to create a circle of positive friends. Remember, if your motivation is low, you may also have negative feelings. That is a good time to listen and borrow some positive energy from others, but do not drain them. You must recharge as soon as possible, because they will expect the same from you. We all need a little re-charging every now and then.

7. **Go Out and Have Fun** – Adults spend so much time being grown-up and serious, until we forget to release the childlike part of ourselves and have fun. When your motivation goes down or you get stuck when trying to achieve your plan, it is time to release your creative ability. Sometime, motivation is lost when things are not going in the direction we had hoped they would go. When that happens it can be difficult to find the answers needed to get back on track. Just take a break! Taking a day to do nothing or to have fun will

make you feel better and you will be surprised at how many solutions will come to mind. Learn to lighten up and laugh as much as you can!

Using the suggestions mentioned will help you stay in the success game until you achieve your dreams. Motivation is a important to realizing any vision that you have for your life. Whenever, you get a little down, refer back to this page and chose one of the items from the list and get started today.

CDs and MP3s for Listening

Below is a recommended list of compact discs or mp3 downloads you should listen to for the next 30 days. Listen to something new off the list everyday for the next 30 days. If you do not have any of these CDs or Mp3s you can purchase come of them at www.shop.designingyourlifetoday.com, purchase at least two from each category and listen to them over and over for 30 days, then map out your plan to acquire the rest of the CDs and Mp3s.

We also have a series of Mp3s that will help you grow and achieve your goals. You can **place an order** from our website at www.shop.designingyourlifetoday.com .

Mental

1. Think & Grow Rich
   by Napoleon Hill
2. Gaining the Confidence to Win
   by Pat Council
3. Men are from Mars/Women are from Venus, by Dr. John Gray
5. Lifetime of Riches
   by Napoleon Hill
6. It's Your Time
   by Pat Council
7. Don't Deny Your Destiny
   by Pat Council
8. The Instant Millionaire
   by Mark Fisher

Physical

1. 8 Weeks to Optimum Health
   by Andrew Weil, MD
2. Eat Smart
   by Robert Haas
3. Use Your Brain to Change Your Age Dr. Daniel Amen

Spiritual

1. Path to Love Deepak Chopra
2. Stress Reduction & Creative Meditations, by Marc Allen
3. The Path
   by Laura B. Jones
4. Manifest Your Destiny
   by Wayne Dyer
5. 7 Spiritual Laws of Success
   by Deepak Chopra
6. Contact Your Inner Guide
   by Shakti Gawain
7. Take Control by Letting Go
   by Pat Council

Mp3s can be purchased at www.shop.designingyourlifetoday.com
Also, get more recommendation by visiting:
www.designingyourlifetoday.com

Power Tip: Do not miss a day of listening. If you do miss a day, double up, so you will stay on track. After you have listened to all the Information on the list, start over and listen to each tape until the end of the 30-day period.

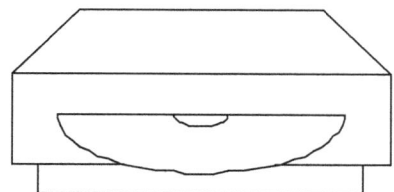

You Need A Little Music

All music is designed to give you some kind of feeling or to stimulate a thought. The kind of feeling you get will be based on the kind of music you choose. Some music can help you think better and provide a base to help you think of logical solutions to problems, for example some music by Mozart. Music can also help reduce stress and calm inner turmoil. Since you are working to improve various aspects of your life, and tastes in music vary, we have listed the guidelines for choosing your music. Follow the guidelines and list the kind of music you would most like to hear. All music titles listed are examples of music that I sometimes listen to. Although there is no specific category for classical music, please feel free to add your favorite classical music, as long as it fits into the guidelines listed below. For example: Mozart is a great piece to listen to when you need to be motivated or stimulate your thinking; therefore Mozart would be listed under the motivational category.

Guidelines:

1. Music should contain clean lyrics, no vulgarity and only positive inspirational language (for instrumentals, the music should excite, motivate, or inspire you).

2. Choose more than one song for each category.

3. Make sure you understand the message in the song or the song has a message you can interpret to fit your needs. Even instrumentals convey a message.

4. Music should inspire you to visualize yourself doing positive things or put some pep in your step.

(List as many songs as you would like.)

Motivational	*Simply Fun*	*Inspirational/Spiritual*
I believe I can Fly	I Feel Good, James Brown	His Eye is on the Sparrow
Walking on Sunshine	_____	_____
_____	_____	_____
_____	_____	_____

Power Tip: Do not underestimate the power of music. Listening to some "get up and go" music on those mornings when you just cannot seem to get into the swing of things can really give you the boost you need. Of course, be sure to include some prayer & meditation before you move forward with the day's events. Music makes a great replacement for the morning news.

Letting Go of Negativity

We are surrounded by negativity on a daily basis. The news, the internet, the radio, and now, it can even be downloaded onto your cell phone. The problem with negative information is that it presents a distorted picture of life and limits one's ability to see a positive or workable solution. Absorbing too much negativity can lead to a belief system that is counterproductive to achieving a set goal. There are some things that can be done to control the amount of negativity that is absorbed into one's life.

> I. **<u>Be honest with yourself</u>**— First of all, it is easy to get away from or limit negativity in your life if you are not a negative person, so start with yourself. Determine whether you are a negative person or not. That may not be easy, because most negative people don't know they are negative. They view their negativity as just stating the facts or as just being honest. Listed below are a few questions that can help you determine if you are a negative person:
>
> 1. Do you have low self-esteem? (We have a section on self-esteem included in this action guide.)
>
> 2. Do you complain constantly?
>
> 3. Do you put down friends or acquaintances that are working at doing better?
>
> 4. Do you constantly complain about all the things you don't like? For example, foods, other people's habits/behavior, types of activities?
>
> 5. Do you accept people as they are or do you always criticize them?

6. If you were assigned to work on a project with others, would you be the one most likely to point out the problems or recommend solutions?

7. Are you always talking about what you don't have?

8. Do you expect to fail, before you even get started? (For example, you say things like, "That will never work," or "It's a waste of time")

9. Are you always alone because you have no friends?

10. Are you always saying that you don't like being around people or that you don't like people to come to your home?

11. Do you criticize other people for being happy about something?

12. Do you think you are a know-it-all and put down other people's ideas?

If you answer yes to more than 3 or more of these questions, you need to work on releasing some of your negative energy.

II. Letting go of Negativity

1. **Begin by writing down some of your positive qualities** (save this list for the "I am" exercise).

2. **Write out 3 positive affirmations.** For example, "Today I will say only positive things."

3. **Spend some quality time with yourself.** (See the "One Fine Day" exercise.)

4. **Embrace and recognize the beauty of nature**:

    A.) Go for a walk and breathe in fresh air.

    i. Visit a flower shop and marvel at the beautiful colors of the many flowers; take the time to smell a few roses (you may even want to buy some and place them on your night stand in your bedroom).

    ii. Awaken early and watch the sunrise, then smile because you are alive to see it.

    iii. Write down some of the things you can do to recognize and embrace all the wonderful gifts that God has allowed nature to present to you. For example: You could walk in the rain or walk barefoot on the beach (wade in the water).

5. **Read at least one motivational book a month.** (Read more than one if you are a fast reader.) (See the recommended reading list in this action guide.)

6. **Limit the number of times you watch the news each week.** Also, limit the number of crime, horror and heavy drama shows or movies you watch. Try watching comedy, romance and self-help shows (you can find many excellent shows on PBS, Public Broadcasting Station). **If you must watch talk shows, watch the ones that have information that will help**

you improve and stay away from the high drama reality shows or talk shows.

7. **Join a club or organization**—make sure the club or organization you join is one where you can help others or it has lots of personal growth for you, such as "Toastmasters". There is nothing more gratifying and uplifting than being able to help someone in need.

8. **Find a job you like**—if you are doing a job you don't like everyday that can definitely be a de-motivator. Map out a plan and start doing what you like. You will definitely change your attitude to a more positive one.

9. **Get away from negative people**—enough said!

10. **Work on becoming more spiritual.** Spend more time seeing how you measure up to the laws in the Bible. You may also want to spend some time in quiet.

SELF-ESTEEM

Way back when you were younger,
Praise was the thing for which you hungered.
But instead of praise others were mean,
And that only lowered your self-esteem.
Now you're grown-up and things turn out bad,
All because of the praise you never had.
But don't you worry, all is not lost,
Cause now that you're grown, you're the boss.
So look in the mirror and in your eyes put a gleam,
To start winning, just raise your self-esteem.

Write your thoughts about this poem:

"I AM…"
(WHO ARE YOU?)

Today is a great day to refine your goals and destiny by creating your "I am" list. To achieve your goals you must have an idea about who you are or who you would like to become. This not only defines your goals, but also your value system. As you think, so shall you become, but also you will not let any thing interfere with the plan you have for you life if it does not fit. If you are not who you would like to become, still write it on your list, but write your phrase in the pretense form, for example: "I am more organized." "I am gentle." Be sure to daily affirm both who you are and who you are becoming. As you affirm each "I am" statement imagine that you are already who you say you are and begin to act that way.

How to Use Your List: Once you have created your "I am" list make 3 copies and put them in the following places: On the refrigerator, the mirror you frequently look into, and keep one with you to read daily at lunchtime or whenever you have a break.

Creating Your "I Am" Power List: Find a time when you will not be interrupted. Number a blank sheet of paper from 1 thru 10 (A blank sheet with numbers has been included for your convenience. See the next page.) Write down all the positive things you think you are or what you wish to become (see example below). Do not hold back or be shy about writing down good thoughts about yourself. If you don't think you have good qualities or acknowledge that you want to acquire some, no one else will.

Remember, while writing your list also include positive qualities you do not exhibit, but would like to adopt. Write the qualities down as though they are already a part of your personality or daily life. If you do not already possess the quality, use an action verb to indicate what you desire to be like. Talk as though it is already happening. For example, use going, becoming, learning, etc.. Then continuously act as you already have the qualities you desire.

Even though we suggested numbering 1 through 10, feel free to make your list as long as necessary. You should try to do this in one sitting, but if you cannot, write your list as things come to mind, but try to complete your list in two days or less. Then start behaving in a manner that is in alignment with your list.

Sample "I Am" List
1. I am kind
2. I am becoming healthy
3. I am friendly
4. I am becoming prosperous

Power Tip: Before you can move in a positive direction, you must have some idea about who you are and who you want to become. Your goal sheet can help with your vision of who you want to become. Really, give you some thought. What do you really want your personality to be like? How would you like the world to perceive you?

Note: If it takes you longer than two days to complete your "I am" list, continue working on it, but go on to the next exercise. It is important that you do not fall too far behind.

I AM

1.

2.

3.

4.

5.

6.

7.

8.

9.

10.

Write your positive comments about yourself. If you would like to make a few notes, feel free to do so below:

Bringing Out the Winner in You!

Reading is definitely fundamental. If you want to release real power to achieve, taking in new information is one of your best and most important options. On the following page you will find a recommended reading list. Throughout this book, you have been asked not to skip certain tasks. Reading some or all of the books on this list, is definitely a must. Have you ever heard the old saying, "garbage in, garbage out"? There is a lot of truth to that saying. Whatever has gone in through your eyes, ears, and even your sense of touch, taste, and smell has helped to shape your thinking and the level of expectation you currently have for your life. For example, If you have been surrounded by negative people and in an impoverish environment, like it or not, you have developed a level of comfort with that kind of atmosphere. It has also established certain belief systems in you that may be preventing you from being your best or using your talents to build a life full of powerful, productive, positive energy. Although an impoverished world is self-defeating and it constantly attacks the sense of self-worth, until people learn something different, this world remains an accepted reality. The world that surrounds you can convince you that you are powerless to make any changes. If no new or contrary information is ingested through reading, the "garbage" keeps piling in and you continue to feel mentally, physically, and spiritually weaker until sometimes thoughts of hopelessness become a part of a daily routine.

Reading the right books helps to convince the mind that there are other alternatives and great possibilities for achieving goals and dreams. Reading is also a great way to keep positive ideas constantly flowing through your mind and no matter what the day has been like the right book can brighten things up or provide solutions. If everyone in your environment is bringing negative ideas, actions, and words, your alternative is the reading list. The books on the reading list contain information that will introduce you to the positive side of life and if you keep reading them, you will stay there. As you take in more positive information, any negative thoughts or hopeless feelings will be replaced by positive thoughts, and positive solutions.

Take your time and read the books on the list. You will notice that the Bible is first on the list. Make sure you read scriptures from the Bible every day. You may go on to read other books on the list, but always take the time to read from the Bible. If you do not know where to start, start from the beginning or start with Proverbs, then go back to the beginning. The recommendation to read the Bible is not about religion. It contains answers to many of the issues people encounter and it is an interesting read.

It is important that you always read something positive, even after the 30-day period is up. Remember, the information you take in today, will shape who you will become tomorrow.

Consider keep a list of all the books you read, just to see how many books you can read in one year. If you are keeping a journal record any changes that have occurred in your way of thinking, especially during the 30-day period.

Reading List

Reading one book a month will broaden your horizons and give you a clearer vision about your life and better directions toward achieving your goals and living your dreams:

1. The Holy Bible
2. Think and Grow Rich — Napoleon Hill
3. Life Visioning — Michael Beckwith
4. The Dynamic Laws of Prosperity — Catherine Ponder
5. Men are From Mars/Women are From Venus — Dr. John Gray
6. How to Win Friends & Influence People — Dale Carnegie
7. Power of Positive Thinking — Norman Vincent Peale
8. Tough Times Don't Last Tough People Do — Dr. Robert Schuller
9. Live Your Dreams — Les Brown
10. The Laws of Prosperity — E. Bernard Jordan
11. The Winner Within — Pat Riley
12. Million Dollar Habits — Robert J. Ringer
13. Look Out For #1 — Robert J. Ringer
14. The Millionaire Moses — Catherine Ponder
15. The Millionaire Joshua — Catherine Ponder
16. Fit For Life — Harvey/Marilyn Diamond
17. Creative Visualization — Shakti Gawain
18. Creating True Prosperity — Shakti Gawain
19. Anger Kills — Virginia Williams
20. Take Time for Your Life — Cheryl Richardson
21. Power of the Soul — John Holland
22. It only takes a minute to change your life — Willie Jolley
23. First Things First — Stephen Covey
24. Living Without Losing — Don Polston
25. Seven Habits of Highly Effective People — Stephen Covey
26. The Energy of Money — Dr. Maria Nemeth
27. Use Your Brain to Change Your Age — Dr. Daniel Amen

Exercise: Read as many books on the list above, in one month, as you can.

Understanding Cause and Effect

You are responsible for whatever condition or state your life is in today. It sounds harsh, but it is true. Not because I say so, but because the "law of attraction" clearly states that you attract who you are and that thoughts become things. You may be reading this with disbelief wondering, how could anyone be responsible for the situations that occur in your life? For example, if someone is in a co-dependent or abusive relationship, it is reasonable to think that no one would want to be in that type of misery. The truth is, they most likely do not want the misery, but getting what you want is more about how you think and who you are than about "wanting". The abusive relationship comes about probably because the person was looking for a rescuer. If someone needs a rescuer, that means they think and feel like a victim; therefore, they often get victimized. The key is to be aware of thoughts and actions. Every action that is taken is a seed that is planted that will bring about a specific result.

In other words, the choices you make today will determine what your life will be like tomorrow. "As you sow, so shall you reap." If you have excessive debt, it may be that you chose to live a life that exceeds your income. You failed to save for emergencies or you chose to work outside your purpose; therefore, your income does not match the lifestyle you are trying to live. The **cause** is poor choices and the **effect** is excessive debt.

Improving your life or getting what you want can be as simple as **thinking before you act or "seeking wise council".** How many things are you doing unconsciously because it has become a habit in your life? Instead of acting without thought, take the time to look at what you are about to do. Do not allow **instant gratification** to lead you toward a future that you may find extremely undesirable and sometimes painful. Consider looking at your life to determine what choices you are making that continue to give you results that make you miserable or leave you wanting. Write those choices down and then write down the choices you know you should be making that will give you the things you desire. Promise yourself that you will think about the consequences of your actions, before you act. Cause and effect is simple to understand. Here's an example: if you choose a mate based only on physical or material (money) reasons, because you did not look for true compatibility, you could eventually find yourself in an unhappy relationship. The **cause** is a choice made using superficial, non-spiritual reasoning. The **effect** is unhappiness and possibly divorce.

Whether we choose to admit it or not, we are solely responsible for the outcome of our lives. Does this mean we do not need help from others? Of course not! We all need each other in one way or another. If someone gets sick, there is a fire, needs therapy, spiritual development or even just a friend, we need help from others. That still does not negate the fact that you are the overseer of your overall standard of living, relationships, and health. For every action there will be some kind of reaction. It is up to you to put you best forward and get the outcome you want. Although, you will not be able to control every outcome exactly the way you would like, putting out the right kind of energy, operating under a strong value system and believing for the best will bring you the best outcome and a well thought out properly planned out action will often produce the results you desire. What you receive from life will be determined by the choices you make. Before you act, consider the consequences and choose wisely, because whatever you do in the present will affect your future. Never forget "there is power in the present moment."

Power Tip: Remember to use cause and effect if you want to receive abundance, "Give and it shall be given unto you." The Bible tells us that if we give first we will receive. I can remember when I used to make fun of the biblical quote, "It is better to give than receive." I would tell everybody that it was better to give to me, because it was always better for me to receive. In other words, I was always looking to take from others. During that time period in my life, I had excessive debt and I was very unhappy.

While we are on the subject of **cause** and **effect**, if you want to begin receiving more, learn to give more. The Bible tells us to "give and it shall be given unto you." It also says, "It is better to give than receive." Both biblical quotes contain two very important keys to how you can receive your abundance and they really work so complete every thing in this exercise. I have met people who love to give and those who do not. It is clear that the givers have more abundance and a more fulfilled life. They seem more content because they have blessed someone with their giving and because they have received their blessings tenfold. On the other hand, I have met the non-givers who were judgmental about giving in their life. They complained while giving and I watched them have no prosperity. They lived with their complaint in poverty and misery. The laws that apply to giving will work for anyone who follows them. If you give with the right intention, you will get a return you could not possibly imagine.

Cause and Effect

1. Make a list of any situations in your life that have not turned out the way you expected:

   _____
   _____
   _____

2. Make a list of any excessive debt you have:_____
   _____
   _____

3. Look at your lists in number 1 and 2 above. Now write down why you think you have had undesirable outcomes in all situations, including excessive debt:

   _____
   _____

4. What could you have done differently?

   _____
   _____

5. What should you do differently now, to make each situation better or to get the desired outcome, next time.

   _____
   _____
   _____

6. On a scale of 1 to 10 (10 being the highest), rate yourself as a giver. _____

7. On a scale of 1 to 10 (10 being the highest), rate yourself as a receiver.

   _____

8. Do you need to give more? _____

   a. Will you give more? If yes, when will you begin and what will you give?

   _____
   _____
   _____

Hint: Give more of whatever you want. If you want more love, give love. If you want more money, give money by donating or making a purchase that will benefit someone.

9. Once you start to give more, write any positive changes that occur in your life, in your journal. If it doesn't happen right away, keep giving, it will happen.

Problem Solving (Excuse Sheet)

Write down every excuse you could possibly have for not making an immediate decision to start on the road toward achieving your goals and dreams. Take a sheet of paper or feel free to write in your journal and start writing every excuse you can remember giving as a reason why you did not complete something. (If you are having a challenge completing this part of the exercise, simply look at your life today. Are you where you want to be in your life? If not, right down the reasons why. In most cases, the reasons will be your excuses. After you have written down every excuse read it out loud along with the statement at the bottom of your excuse page. Once you have finished, complete the problem-solving page then, tear your excuses up and throw them into the garbage. For a greater impact you may want to burn your excuses before discarding them. No matter how you get rid of that piece of paper, make sure you passionately rip them out of this book, your notebook, or journal and destroy them. Excuses are worth nothing; therefore, they have no place in your life, if you want to achieve your goals!

Examples of an excuse sheet

The excuses I have for not achieving my goals are:

> I am married
> I am not married
> I have children
> I am too old
> I don't have enough money

Power Tip: Recognize that once you have destroyed your excuse sheet, this represents mentally removing any obstacle that has been preventing you from going toward success. The only thing stopping you from realizing your dreams is you. Nothing can stop you, if you choose to excel and remain committed to achieving your goals.

Excuse Sheet

Feel free to write down as many excuses as you can think of.

The excuses I have for not achieving my goals are:

Read Aloud: *I have allowed the above ridiculous excuses to hold me back for too long. My first step for breaking through these excuses is by destroying this piece of paper that holds all my old excuses. From this day forward, nothing will hold me back.*

Another Reminder: Tear this up only after you have completed the problem-solving page.

Problem Solving (Eliminating Your Excuses)

This exercise is designed to help you start working through the excuses that you may have been using to stop you from traveling down the road of success. Make sure you complete this exercise without interruptions from television, music, or the ringing telephone.

Instructions: Take your excuse sheet and on the problem solving page write down as many solutions as you can. Each solution will help cancel out the excuses you came up with. If you cannot come up with solutions on your own, ask someone whose opinion you value (Make sure they are positive and understand about success.). Once you have written several solutions, choose the solution that best fits the excuse and set a date to take action. Remember to disregard all negative answers.

Example: The self-defeating excuses I have allowed to exist in my heart and mind have prevented achievement of my goals, but implementing the solutions I have written below will help me move forward to success in my chosen project:

Excuse	**Solution**
I am married	I will talk to my spouse and ask his/her support. If my spouse will not support me, I will be true to myself. My spouse's true love for me will allow him/her to respect my decision.

Power Tip: Write down as many solutions as you feel you need to. Use the next page and add a separate sheet of paper if it is needed, but write until each excuse has been eliminated and you are moving forward with achieving your set goals. Seek help from a positive friend if you feel you need it, but always remember to follow your heart.

Problem Solving

The self-defeating excuses I have created for not achieving my goals can be easily solved by implementing the solutions I have written below:

Excuse   **Solution**

Read Aloud:
My problems have been solved and my excuses eliminated. I am on my way to achieving my goals. I am free of any obstacle that once prevented me from moving forward. I feel fantastic, because I am on my way to winning!

- Save this page and read it whenever you need a reminder.

Quotes To Read Daily

All of the quotes listed below are positive and thought provoking. Do not rush through reading these quotes. Pick a different quote each day, read it, and think about its true meaning. Take the time to figure out how the quote can be applied to your life and what it means in relation to your goals and desire lifestyle. (Make sure you study each quote.) If you do not understand how the quotes relate to you, seek advice or help from a spiritual advisor.

1. "As a man thinketh, so is he."

2. "As you sow, so shall you reap."

3. "…and this too shall pass away."

4. "The quality of your life is in direct proportion to your commitment to excellence."

5. "Anything the mind of man can conceive and believe it can achieve."

6. "Attitude is Everything."

7. "Never, Never Quit."

8. "Tough times don't last, tough people do."

9. "If there is no struggle, there is no progress."

10. "The future is purchased by the present."

11. "We learn from failure much more than success."

12. "I always view problems as opportunities in work clothes."

13. "All men who have achieved great things have been dreamers."

14. "Man's mind once stretched by a new idea, never regains it's original dimensions."

15. "There is no achievement without goals."

16. "We are continually faced by great opportunities brilliantly disguised as insoluble problems."

17. "What force is more potent than love."

18. "The best way to cheer yourself is to try cheering up somebody else."

19. "Prefer a loss to dishonest gain; the one brings pain at the moment, the other for all time."

20. "Great minds must be ready not only to take opportunities, but to make them."

21. "Those who bring sunshine to the lives of others can not keep it from themselves."

22. "No one is useless in this world who lightens the burden of another."

23. "For the resolute and determined there is time and opportunity."

24. "Many receive advice, only the wise profit from it."

25. "Doubt whom you will, but never yourself."

26. "Opportunity…often it comes in the form of misfortune, or temporary defeat."

27. "Success doesn't come to you…you go to it."

28. "The soul that has no established aim loses itself."

29. "Success is not a journey, it's a destination."

30. "There is no success without hardship."

31. "If you don't know where you're going, how do you expect to get there?"

Visualization

Visualization is a necessary part of goal achievement, because you become what you think about. In order to go to the next level, you must have a visual picture of where you want to go. It is not necessary to know how you will get to where you want to go, but having a vision will put you on the right track for success. It also shows that you are willing to take responsibility for the direction of your life.

Exercise: This exercise should be done in conjunction with your commitment board or you can simply allow your memory to serve you, but it works best with your board. Look at a picture on your commitment board and start visualizing yourself as an active part of that picture.

For Example: If you have a picture of a house on your commitment board, imagine yourself already in the house. See yourself walking through each room. What size are the rooms? What kind of furniture do you have in the rooms? See yourself taking a bath in your new bathtub. Make your visualization as graphic and detailed as possible.

Power Tip: This exercise should be done everyday during your quiet time. Visualize the scenes for your life that you would like to make a reality. Always see yourself playing an active role in each one of your dreams. Remember, your imagination is your gift to be used to attract the perfect life for you, so do not be afraid to dream.

If you are having a hard time visualizing big dreams, start by seeing small things. Imagine that you are driving a better car or earning $200.00 more a week. Once you feel comfortable picturing small goals, move on to bigger and better dreams!

Optional: Once you have completed your visualization exercise, you may want to write down some of your visions and read them a few days later. We have provided you with a blank page in case you decide to write your thoughts down or you may write in your journal. Although, you have written your thoughts down, it is important to visualize your goals everyday during your quiet time.

Visualization (Blank Page for your ideas)

Self-Talk and Affirmations

One of the reasons change may be difficult is because of the undesirable and self-defeating habits that are kept alive through mental and verbal reinforcement. Negative things that are spoken about often have a way of becoming an unwanted part of our lives. If someone constantly says that they are not good at math, constantly affirming that phrase would eventually make it come true for them. They would begin to have a difficult time with mathematics. That is why it is very important to be aware of what is being affirmed into your life. The best way to stay in tuned with what's being spoken into your life is to practice daily affirmations.

Exercise: Write down all the self-talk that you find yourself using. Write down both positive and negative talk. Also, write down what you say about others, that is a form of self-talk, too. What you say about others is your view of the world and yourself. Be conscious of your conversation for an entire day. Listen for phrases such as the one's listed below:

      I am so stupid
      I can't do anything right
      I don't look good in that
      I'm not good at _____
      I am so clumsy
      I've been like this my whole life
      I hate Mondays, things always go wrong

Once you have written down the things you normally say, read over that list and keep only the positive comments. If there are no positive comments, write down positive comments to replace the negative ones and focus on saying those, instead of what you have always been saying. From now on, continue to focus on the positive comments only. Do not refer to your "I Am" list when creating your new list of positive affirmations. Once your list has been completed, then compare it to your "I Am" list. Did you list the same qualities or do you have some new qualities on this list that are not on your "I Am" list? Add the new qualities to your "I Am" list. The positive comments written below should give you some idea as to the type of phrases to write to replace your old way of thinking:

> I am becoming very smart
> I do things much better
> It's okay to make a mistake sometimes
> I look good in different styles of clothing
> I am capable of doing many things well.

Begin saying good things to yourself. You will eventually change how you look at yourself and how you look at life. You will also respond to others in a more positive manner.

Affirmations: Using your "I Am" List, daily affirm that you are the person you have written about on your list. This will only work if you truly want to become that person and begin to act the part.

Power Tip: When creating the list, remember to be conscious of the negative comments you say to others, especially children and other members of your family. The comments will not only have a negative and long lasting effect on them, it will defeat your effort to develop a better you. What you say about others is a good indication of how you feel about yourself.

Lighten Up!

No matter what goals you set, if you are not having fun while working to achieve them, it is not worth the effort. All work and no play makes Jane a dull girl and Jack a dull boy. Make sure do not become too busy to take the time to have fun. Life is supposed to be lived to the fullest. That means, taking some time away from work to have fun and relax. Sometimes people call their work, play. That is wonderful that they love what they are doing for a living, but playing and working is not the same thing. They require different types of energy. One is considered down time, because that's when it is time to re-charge, so when work time rolls around, mind and body are ready to go. That would be playtime or fun time. The other requires intense focus and it is mostly a release of energy or a transfer of energy toward the goal or project that is being worked on, daily.

Having fun is about connecting with family and friends and transferring energy, but also receiving energy back into your life. It means sharing entertaining and fun activities with those who only require that you express yourself by enjoying their company. By the way, having fun does not mean you should always do everything that everyone else wants. It means doing some kind of sport or recreational activity that you enjoy doing, also. Your mental and emotional recovery is important to your success, so be sure to add something that you like doing, as well as indulging and including love ones.

No human being is meant to work all the time. It does not matter whether you work for a corporation, small business, yourself, or if you work at home raising a family. You are still to take a break and have fun.

Part of having fun includes laughter. How much do you laugh on daily basis? If you have a hard time answering this question, then you are not laughing enough. Laughter is good for your health and it helps you think more clearly. It also, gives you an energy boost. The more you laugh, the clearer your mind becomes and then you can actually achieve more. Laughter also creates intimacy between you and those you are laughing with and it generates a consistent feeling of happiness. The saying laughter is the best medicine is true. Laughter can improve the function of your blood vessels and increase the flow of blood to your heart, so your heart will be healthier. Laughter also triggers the release of endorphins, the body's natural feel-good chemical which promotes an overall sense of well-being and boost your immune system. (Taken from HelpGuide.org). If you consider work to be play, then consider this. Constantly, working does not come with the health benefits that fun and laughter bring, so do your self a favor and lighten up.

TURN THE PAGE NOW AND TAKE ACTION!

One Fine Day (A Fun Day)

Today is a great day to let your guard down and be like a kid again or just pick a day to do nothing but have fun. It does not matter where you live, there is some place you can go or something you can do to have fun. **Do not** come up with any excuses for not having fun. Grab a friend or your family and get to it. Today is not a workday! Simply take the time and be good to yourself by relaxing and add some laughter in throughout the day. Make this request your only option. You do not need a lot of money. If you cannot figure out what to do, we have supplied a list of suggestions.

Caution: Do not watch the news or read the newspaper today. Take a break from all the sensationalism. It will still be there for you, tomorrow. I promise. Today is going to be a stress free, fun-filled day.

Go to the park
Go for a drive to a scenic area
Lounge around all day/watch comedies
Visit a museum or art gallery
Visit an amusement park
Visit a travel agent/plan a trip
Have dinner at your favorite restaurant
Call & talk to your best friends
Spend a day at the Cinema (comedies)
Have your hair done
Get a massage
Play basketball with the family
Play secret agent with water pistols
(Yes, adults play with the pistols, too.)
Play board games

Go to a concert
Go to the beach
Go shopping/spend money
Go window-shopping
Go dancing
Work on a hobby
Take a 3 hour cruise
Go to a party
Play a favorite sport
Buy a new outfit
Get a pedicure
Paint abstract pictures
Have sing-a-longs

Play electronic fun games

(On the next page write down some of your fun ideas.)

Fill in something you've always wanted to do and do it:

Power Tip: Do not do any work today, that includes extended periods of housework or yard work (unless this is your idea of fun).

GRATEFUL

I'm thankful for this very day,
It's nice to be guided, in the right way.
I'm happy that you're there, in everything I do,
I'm grateful to be blessed, over and over by you.
I breathe the fresh air and see the morning sun,
I say a grateful prayer, my blessings have begun.
I see the shimmering moon, now the day is through,
I say another prayer, I'm so grateful to you.

Write down 3-5 things you are grateful for:

1.
2.
3.
4.
5.

A Day of Gratitude and Smiles

Practice giving thanks to God each day for everything that you already have. Today spend it making a list of things you are grateful for. This exercise will help eliminate any thoughts you have about there being a lack of abundance. As you start to make a list of the things that you are grateful for, you will begin to recognize all the wonderful things in your life. Your gratitude will grow and you will begin to attract more into your life. Gratitude releases the kind of power needed prepare us to be mentally ready to accept the things we believe deserve. Concentrate on this exercise and do your best to fill up the next page. You will find you have many reasons to be grateful.

Exercise: Write down as many reasons as you can think of for being grateful. You may carry this workbook, your notebook, or a sheet of paper around with you and as things come to you throughout the day, write them down. Once you have completed your list, read your list out loud. Begin by reading the statement that precedes your list and end by reading the last statement on the page.

Examples of Gratitude: I am grateful for:

My life	My strength to look for a job
My health	The courage to fulfill my dreams
My job	My family
My business	Good friends

Power Tip: If you have not been doing so, start today by giving thanks for your life, and give thanks each time you have a meal. Continue to show your gratitude by saying thank you to anyone who does something for you whether you asked for it or not. Completing this task alone could bring positive things into your life.

*Today you have learned the **art of gratitude,** continue it always.

A Day of Gratitude and Smiles

"On this day and always, I am grateful to God for all he has given to me. Because I am grateful I dedicate this day as my day of gratitude and I have taken the time to list all those things for which I am grateful."

Write your grateful thoughts here.

I am grateful for:

"All the things I have listed above lets me know that, I am loved by God and that he has a special purpose for my life. I will continue to give thanks each day and add things to my list as I notice them. Today, I have discovered a better

meaning of life, and because of that I feel closer to God and the power he has instilled in me. The day is done."

Now, smile and from this day forward you will begin and end each day being grateful for who you are and what you have.

The Joy of Life

(The Power behind Purpose)

If you wake up everyday feeling frustrated and empty on the inside, it may be because you are not living up to your true purpose in life. A strong indication that someone is not living out their passionate is that they dread getting up and going to work on Monday mornings or any other day for that matter. The complaining begins and happens often. We were all born with unique qualities that would allow each of us to serve a special purpose in life. As a children, many of us probably began living our purposes by automatically taking an interest in one thing more than the other or often daydreaming about pursuing a special task as a grown up. Sometimes with excitement, as children we shared our passion with an adult who scoffed at the idea or belittled the situation by saying, "You're too young to know what you want."
Eventually, the living environment took over and as some became adults, they allowed the passion for their purpose to slip away. Life became about simply making a living or doing whatever it took to get by in life, because of mental conditioning from childhood. Fear is also another factor that caused many to forsake their purposes. Instead more time was spent being dedicated to everyone else, except themselves. Does any of this sound like you? Are you living your purpose, today? If you are not living your purpose, this marks the beginning and continuation of most of the dissatisfaction within your life and your daily works. Whenever you live someone else's dream or fulfill a purpose other than your own, you limit your ability to excel and smother the inner power needed to create the kind of life you have always wanted and deserved. To become a winner, to be satisfied and reach your goals in life, you must find your

true purpose and then take steps to bring your purpose into reality. Start walking in your purpose by taking action to do what it takes to manifest your destiny. If you have no idea what your purpose is or how to begin searching, consider using the following steps:

1. **Write your thoughts down**. Find a blank sheet of paper or use your journal and begin to write down some of the things you like doing. Only focus on the things you would like to be doing, not the amount of money you would like to make. Write down as many ideas as you like. Write down what excites you.

2. **Choose one of them.** After completing your list, pick the one thing you would like to do everyday, if you never had to worry about money.

3. **If you have no answers, spend some quiet time alone** and meditate on your purpose. You may have buried your dream out of fear or out of the disappointment of never having taken steps to do the one thing in life that brought you true peace and happiness. Meditating for a few days or weeks will bring your true passion back to life. Keep a pad and pen next to your bed, the answer could come at anytime and when it does, make sure you write it down.

4. **If you still have no answers.** What are people always telling you that you are good at doing? What are others always saying you should be doing for a living? Write those down and then meditate and pray for guidance.

Discovering your purpose and making a decision to live your dream will give you more power than you ever thought you had. You will wake up each day feeling more alive and happy. You will embark on a journey toward success and even if you feel fear, your passion to live your dream will push you forward toward achievement. You will want to share more of yourself with others and your heart and mind will guide you in the right direction. You will begin to feel closer to God, because you will have discovered your purpose and a part of His will for your life. That which seemed like a painful struggle and tedious work will be transformed into play and complete joy for life. You may still have some struggles as you begin to live your passion, but you will have fun and be excited about the challenges you are confronted with.   Most importantly, you will understand the meaning of "endless possibilities." The limitations that once dictated your life will be lifted. The prosperity you might have longed for will fall at your feet. The idea of giving and receiving will increase in your thoughts and your reality, thereby bringing more into your life than you ever imagined. The pressure constantly felt from living a life without purpose will be transformed into a life filled with light, love, and an indescribable sense of peace and happiness. You will learn that you can have the things you desire all because you obey your spirit within and started carrying out a purpose.

People without a purpose will eventually suffer from a loss of imagination and lose their zest for life. Loss of those things creates mediocrity, a feeling of emptiness, and sometimes poverty. You have been given the power to bring ideas and thoughts into reality. A power given only to mankind, so today is a great day to look in the mirror and release the power you have within. I have had several people come up to me at the end of one of my seminars with a look of agony and tell me that they really have no clue as to what their purpose is. My response has always been the same. I tell them, "Everybody knows what they want to do or become, they just don't want to admit that they know because they are afraid of ridicule from others, they fear failure, or they think that once they admit that they really know what they want to do and they do nothing about it, then they would have to live with their slothfulness and they would know that they have failed themselves."

What Is Your Life's Purpose?
(More about Life's Purpose)

Until you discover your true purpose in life, you will be out of sync with the universe and this would account for some of the unhappiness or emotional turmoil, you might feel. This exercise is designed to help put you on the path to realizing your true purpose in life and maybe even cause you to make the decision to unlock the door to your world of complete fulfillment.

Exercise: Answer all the questions on the next pages and follow all instructions carefully. Do not allow your answers to be guided by fear. In order for this exercise to be effective, you must be honest. This is your personal action guide, so answer from the heart. Do this exercise without interruptions, if possible. Write down as many answers as you would like. If more than one answer comes to mind for each question, write it down. Today you may break the rules by relaxing your structured life. Let your mind go and have fun while answering each question! There are no wrong answers. Some questions may sound repetitive, answer them anyway.

Power Tip: When searching for your purpose, although you may have completed the exercise, listen to your inner voice. When meditating, different or better answers may come to you, feel free to go back and answer any of the questions again. **Do not** change your original answers. Your purpose will be discovered a lot sooner if you are honest with yourself. Do not judge your answers. Write down the answers that you hear in your mind and feel in your heart. Answer the questions alone. Please do not solicit anyone else's thoughts or opinions.

What Is Your Life's Purpose?

A. Answer the following:

1. If I could be doing anything with my life right now, it would be:
   _____
   _____
   _____

2. Do you sometimes hear an inner voice telling you what you should be doing? Yes or No (circle one). If yes, what does it constantly say?
   _____
   _____
   _____ If no, go to the next question, but don't worry.

3. If I could turn back the hands of time, this is what I would do differently with my life:_____
   _____
   _____

4. If I did not have _____, I would be doing _____ for a living today.

5. If I could _____, I would be doing _____ for a living today.

6. If it were not for _____, I would be a _____ right now.

7. What do you think is stopping you from doing what you would like to do?
   _____
   _____

8. List what you think your natural talents are:_____
   _____
   _____

9. Have you ever given your talents the respect they deserve? (Respect means, have you used your talents as intended?)_____
   _____
   _____

10. People say I am good at:_____
    _____
    _____

11. Do you worry about what others will think of you, if you start to pursue your dreams?_____
_____
_____
_____

12. Do you feel a sense of peace in your life:_____
_____
_____
_____

13. Does your work seem like work or play?_____
_____
_____
_____

14. If you did not have to worry about money, what would you be doing?_____

B. Before you begin meditating each day or night, ask God, "What is the purpose of my life?" Listen for the answer. Keep a pad and a pen next to your bed at night, so if the answer comes to you at 2:00 or 3:00 a.m., you can write it down. Make sure you write anything down that comes to mind, no matter what the time is. Wake up and write!

C. Once you have discovered your purpose, re-read your "I Am" list and consider fulfilling your purpose when writing out your "goals", "plan of action", and "daily to-do list"! You only have one life, live it!

D. Once you have completed exercises A through C, complete the page titled "I know my purpose in life." Write until you feel you have a complete picture in writing.

I Know The Purpose For My Life

My purpose is to:

SELF-ESTEEM

If you ever, ever wonder why,
You can't win, when you try.
When life seems to make you blue,
Cause you always fail at what you do.
If all your projects are a flop,
And you would like to simply stop.
Change the way you look at life,
And you will rid yourself of strife.
Change the way you look at you,
And you will win in all you do.
Remember all you'll ever need,
Is to develop a higher self-esteem.

Write down how you feel about yourself:

The Ultimate Joy of Life
(Love)

Wisdom is a wonderful thing! Money is a wonderful thing! Having perfect health is a wonderful thing, but without love in your life, you have nothing. I once heard someone say love is highly overrated. The truth is . . . it's not rated high enough. Many have bought into the phrase, "What's love got to do with it?" The phrase is used as a negative, but love has everything to do with it! If you want to prosper in life, you must have love. Love is the tree on which all good fruit grows.

Many times people get confused about love and what it really means to us humans. When we hear about love, we think about romance most of the time. Have you ever heard the phrase "romance without finance, ain't nothing?" There is some truth to that. If you want to romance someone, it does take money. Romancing, someone involves buying flowers, candy, wining, and dining, or taking them on romantic trips; however, romance isn't permanent, and it is not love. Love is permanent. In the movie, "The Princess Bride," Princess Buttercup told the evil king that 'no matter what, her Wesley would come for her, because they had true love and true love never dies.' That is true. If you have ever truly loved someone, you will always have feelings of love for that person. Romance is only a part of the "wooing" ritual. He brings you flowers. She prepares a candlelight dinner. Romance is beautiful, it is fun, it feels good, and it may lead to love; however, it can also lead to a temporary love affair that may leave you with a broken heart and disillusioned. The objective is to bask in some forms of romance, but before you go to the next level (sexual or true matters of the heart) make sure that you are getting involved into something that's real and right for both parties involved. How do you know if it's real? Let's just say that marriage would be close or completed.

If you have ever been fooled by romance, it's okay. All you wanted was love and there is nothing wrong with that. The key is to get a better understanding of what love is and to keep in mind that there are different forms of love. There is the love you have for yourself. There is the love you get from children, the love you get from friends, the love you get from family, the love you get from people you help, and the love of God. Usually, the love we have for friends and family is apparent; however, Eros love and self-love may not always be easy to pinpoint. Here is an easy test. What growth is taking place? When love is real, life flourishes. Personal growth takes place and those who interact with you will grow, also. The challenge that comes with recognizing love is that we think that love means everything will be "peaches and cream" or easy going all the time. Some tend to think that there will never be an argument or disagreement. That is a myth. Because love brings personal growth and other types of positive manifestation, we must first uncover that love in each other and sometimes that means "tough love" must come into play. In my opinion, tough love is when we stand our ground based on a positive set of values and principles in order to help someone make the adjustment for their own personal growth or to establish boundaries for ourselves. Although, it is called tough love, this type of love is without judgment of someone's character. In fact, like any love, it lays the foundation for more love to grow. Keep in mind that without love, nothing grows, and the power to get results in your life will be non-existent.

If you are having a difficult time thriving or getting results in your life, then examine your walk with love. How do you feel about yourself and other people in general? How about your love life, are you having difficulty getting love into your life? Maybe it is because your heart is closed because of fear, non-forgiveness, no life's purpose or other things that are preventing your love energy from flowing. Decide to open your heart and give love unconditionally, then you will get love back and you will never be without love, again. If you are searching for the love of a mate, learn to love based on the true meaning of love and you will get all the love you want and need from that special someone. The essence of all human beings is love. In all cases the missing link to massive success is love. That is why it is very important that you love with all your heart. Love others, love what you do for a living, love family and friends and most importantly love yourself and love life.

If you tried it and it did not work the first time try it again, but before you try loving again, consider some of the tips below:

1. **Assess yourself and your last relationship** – Although, the new person in your life has nothing to do with the old relationship, there is one common denominator, YOU! Make sure you take a look at yourself before you place all the blame on the other person, also be fair with yourself, and don't take all the blame, either. See if you can figure out what went wrong. Ask yourself, what fulfillment did you need that you did not get? What was it you could have given, but did not.

2. **Be certain you know what love is** – Although you may have the feelings that come with being in love, the mechanics involved in being with the one you love are more complicated. For example, you have to be unselfish, kind, respectable, patient and a host of other things. If you think you don't know what true love is, the best place

to look is in the Holy Bible. Read 1 Corinthians 13:1 thru 13 verses.

3. **Recall and examine how your parents, guardian, or other members of your family displayed love** – Are your parents divorced? Did you grow up hearing your parents argue all the time? It is important that you determine who taught you about love. Please, do not say you were never taught about love. You learned to love, by what you saw and how you were treated. You may not know the essence of real love, but the goodness is, you can learn it.

4. **How much do you love yourself?** - If you say you love yourself to yourself that is one thing. But if you are constantly saying it to others, then you are trying to convince yourself that you care about you. The way you treat yourself will show you how much you really love yourself. Even more so, the way you treat yourself when no one is looking will give you all the answers about how you feel about you. Consider this, when you do things to prove a point to others, you are only doing it to validate your own worthiness to yourself, and you are longing for others to help you convince yourself that you are worthy of something. It is the same with love, the more talk about how much you love yourself and how great you think you are, the more you are trying to convince you and the world around you that you are worth loving.

No matter what has happened in your life, never stop loving yourself and others. If you have been hurt or someone has wronged you, take some time to heal, make the necessary changes and continue to love. If you think you've forgotten how, watch babies and toddlers. They seem to love unconditionally. They will hug and exhibit kindness just because they can. Pets have also mastered the art of unconditional love. Watch them and take notes, then take action in name of love. That's living. That's joy. That's love!

LOVE AND RELATIONSHIPS

This questionnaire is designed to help you think about your loving relationship with yourself and others. Because there is so much to learn about love and relationships with others, there will be more about love in **Volume II** of the next action guide.

1. If you are a <u>female</u>, how did your mother treat your father or other men? If you are a <u>male</u>, how did your father treat your mother or other women?

2. What is your idea of a loving relationship?

3. What role do you think a man should play in a woman's life? (To be answered by a man or a woman)

4. What role do you think a woman should play in a man's life? (To be answered by a man or a woman)

5. Based on your answers to questions 3 and 4, has your idea of the role each party should play been working in your life?

6. What kind of relationship do you have with other people?

7. If you have any, how do you treat your children?

8. How do your children respond to you?

9. What does love mean to you?

10. Do you think of sex, when you think of a relationship between a man and a woman?

11. Do you think there is something wrong with how you view love and relationships?

12. How do you feel about love and money?

MORE ABOUT LOVE

To get to power, you must release your love for others, for life, and purpose. Finding a purpose and fulfilling it is easier when you have dealt with obstacles that may be preventing you from loving fully. Look at the chart below to identify any obstacles to love that may be preventing your energy from flowing, so you can flourish. For example, <u>unconditional love</u> would be, loving someone, even though you feel they do not deserve it. <u>Write down</u> your thoughts about each category.

WHAT FUELS POWER?

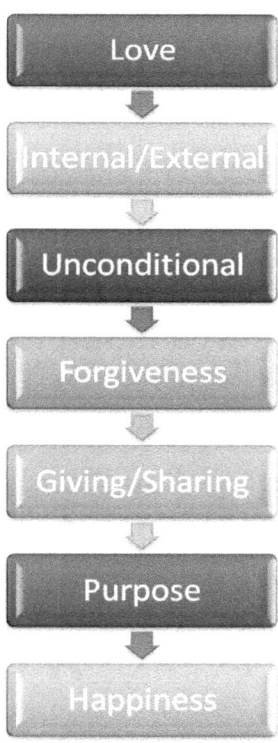

IT'S OKAY TO HAVE SELF-ESTEEM

When we look at the spiritual aspect of things, we learned that we should not over-indulge in "self." That is true; however, paying attention to your self-esteem is not over-indulging in "self." When you are over indulging in "self," you are constantly using your carnal knowledge and you are always catering to the needs of your flesh. When you consider your self-esteem, you are giving attention to the kind of image you have of yourself. You are not looking to become involved in your own "ego stroking" session. You are simply accepting and affirming that you are special. You are also not trying to prove that you are better than other people, you are simply working on restoring or cultivating a feeling of self-worth, so you can, with confidence, fulfill the purpose, which God put you here to serve. Improving your self-esteem is the means by which you, with God's permission, destroy the unhappy and unhealthy image given to you by mankind (a relative, friend, or other people you may have allowed to influence you).

Sometimes, things can be taken too literally. For example, when people tell you it does not matter how you look. "It's what's on the inside that counts." A part of that is true, but the Bible says your "body is a temple." If you are obese to the point where you are unhealthy and unattractive, the outside counts. Consider this. If you have a poor self-image of yourself can you really serve your purpose? What can you do for others?

I have watched so many people shy away from examining their own sense of worthiness, because it involves taking a look at their self-esteem. These are the same people who pray, praise, and profess their faith in God, yet they make no changes. They carry the same disdain for themselves, they always had.

How can anyone who truly believes and has faith in God, think that they are not worthy of receiving the best? You are all entitled to the best that life has to offer. If you do not feel good about the person you are, you will often reject the best and accept the worst things in life, especially if you are not accustomed to receiving the good things in life. It is important that you learn to accept all the good that is offered to you. If you have a hard time accepting things, start by learning to accept compliments. If someone gives you a nice compliment, do not respond with a negative answer, simply smile and say, "thank you." Then constantly remind yourself that you deserve to have someone say nice things about you and that you deserve to receive all the good things that you are offered. Always remember, if you think you deserve to have things, you will receive them.

(Please turn the page and complete all the tasks on the following page.)

Let's Look At Your Self-esteem

Sometimes the main reason for the inability to achieve success is due to a particular thought process. How you feel about yourself; what you see when you look in the mirror and what you think you deserve for your life can affect your desired lifestyle. Now, it is time to discover if you have been acting as your own worst enemy or as your best friend by taking a look at your self-esteem. Referring to the self-talk section will be helpful in this exercise, but do not refer to it until you have completed the exercise on the next page.

You will need a mirror.

Exercise: Complete all the exercises in this section as honestly as you can. Whatever you are feeling as you answer the questions, please allow that feeling to come out and write it down. Then replace those comments with the new positive comments you have created about yourself. Each time you replace a negative phrase with a new positive phrase, read it aloud and look at yourself in the mirror and smile. (It feels funny doesn't it? Don't worry, the funny feeling will pass. Eventually, you will come to like it.) Constantly practice receiving all the new positive ideas about yourself. That is why it is important that you do this exercise in front of your mirror.

Examples of Negative Phrases: "You're so clumsy," "You're stupid," "You're going to be nothing when you grow up."

Power Tip: Once you have identified the negative talk that was instilled in you, make sure you replace it with positive self-talk. As an adult you can now re-create a positive inner picture. Decide what kind of image you would like to have and recognize that you now have it, because it has been identified in your mind. Think about your new image everyday for no less than 30 days. Be sure to write in your journal, how you feel about you.

Take A Look At Your Self-Esteem

1. Think back to when you were a child. What were some of the negative phrases that were used to describe you or your behavior as a kid? Write as many phrases as you like.

   _____   _____
   _____   _____
   _____   _____
   _____   _____

   *Any member of your family, schoolmates, etc. could have said these negative phrases to you. Write down any phrase that you remember which may have had an effect on how you feel about yourself, no matter who said it.

2. How did these phrases make you feel?
   _____

3. Describe any negative feelings or images you may have of yourself. Identify where these feelings came from.
   _____

4. Were the people who made you feel inadequate or "bad inside" justified in making their comments? If yes, why do you feel they were justified?
   _____
   _____

5. Is it possible they were wrong? If no, why not?
   _____

6. Is it possible you were criticized unfairly, because the other person had the problem and not you?

7. Are you hard on yourself when you make a mistake?

8. What do you say to yourself when you make a mistake?

9. Did you have a parent who left you or was abusive to you? Describe how you felt:

10. Did you have a parent who was abusive to himself or herself?

11. Are you able to forgive others for what they did to you in the past?

12. Are you able to forgive yourself for making a mistake?

Part II

1. Going back to Question 1 in Part I, write down what you wish your family or others had said to you (write positive comments only). Write down how you wish you had been treated:

   _____
   _____
   _____
   _____

2. If you could tell the individuals who said or did unpleasant things to you how you feel, what would you say to them? (Say your comments out loud and **pretend** you are talking to them. If you want to tell them they were wrong, tell them. Remember that there is nothing wrong with disagreeing with someone, regardless of his or her relationship to you, as long as it is done with respect. So, speak up with much passion and much respect. It is okay; no one will hear you.)

3. If the other person had the problem, what was their problem? Do you feel it was your fault? If not, then do you recognize that their criticisms of you were invalid and not based on sound logic?

4. It is time to create a new you. After you have completed all the tasks in this section. Turn to the next page and start writing. Once you have completed your new portrait, read it aloud and refer to it often.

5. Depending on your answer to Question 8 in Part I, you may suffer from low self-esteem due to fear or anger. Do not be embarrassed to seek professional help, if you feel you need it.

6. Write letters to anyone who may have hurt you or who you feel may have contributed to your self-image. Make sure you express all your feelings in writing. You may save the letters if you choose, but I suggest you destroy them as soon as you feel you have released the negative feelings. It is time to put the negative behind you and live your life as the confident person you were meant to be. (Refer to the section on Forgiveness.)

You deserve to have the best that life has to offer you, but you will not attract the best if you don't clean up your personal issues. So remember, it is necessary and important to examine and improve your self-esteem.

ATTITUDES

Words can never adequately convey the incredible impact of our attitude toward life.

The longer I live the more convinced I become that life is 10 percent what happens to us and 90 percent how we respond to it.

I believe the single most significant decision I can make on a day-to-day basis is my choice of attitude.

It is more important than my past, my education, my bankroll, my successes or failures, fame or pain, what other people think of me or say about me, my circumstances, or my opinion.

Attitude keeps me going or cripples my progress. It alone fuels my fire or assaults my hope. When my attitudes are right; there's no barrier too high, no valley to deep, no dream too extreme, no challenge too great for me.

Your Self-Portrait

"This is my new self-portrait. (You may now refer to the "I Am" exercise.) I realize that I do not deserve the poor self-image I have. Today I will create the kind of image I deserve to have. This is who I am starting today:"

CHANGE

Change is definite and not by chance,
It can make you frown or dance.
But if some pain with change you've had,
Recognize that change is still not bad.
For if you look closer at change you'll see,
That in it lies a greater opportunity.
So smile when you see the winds of change,
Because it's always good that things don't stay the same.

Write down some of the changes you have made in your life, since you started reading this book:

A Day of Non-Judgment

Today, make the decision that you will spend the day saying only positive things and not passing judgment on anyone. For example, if someone is doing something you do not agree with and it is not affecting you or hurting someone, do not make comments. Do not sit and watch the news, and then label people as "bad". Today make the commitment that, you will not find anything wrong with anyone, instead you will take the time to understand him or her and respect them for being different.

By spending a day of non-judgment, you will release a lot of mental and emotional pressure and have a clearer mind. You will also be able to make stronger, more valuable connections with people. Doing this will help you focus more on your own self-improvement and increase your confidence to achieve your goals.

Exercise: **Do not** judge anyone today. If you make the mistake of passing judgment before the day is done, write down that you made a mistake and then affirm that you will successfully complete this task tomorrow. Start again the next day.

Power Tip: It is important that you successfully complete this task. If you are able to control your constant judgments or comments about others, you will develop the discipline to focus on you and improve your lifestyle with each and everyday.

The objective is to learn not to quickly label people, things, or ideas—in a negative way, especially if you do not have all the facts. Take the time to remove yourself from situations that might cause you to judge others. For example: gossiping with friends or co-workers.

Physical Fitness

Although, I am not a physician or an expert on physical fitness, I have discovered one cold hard truth: If you want to be physically fit, you have to eat right and exercise. I have tried diet pills, fad diets, and diet clinics. You name it; I've tried it, except for surgery or a severe eating disorder (bulimia or anorexia). No matter what I tried, it never remained permanent. I always gained back the weight I lost plus a few more pounds. It was not until I learned to exercise consistently and eat right that I became more physically fit. I have been fighting obesity since I was a teenager. I always joked that I have my fat gene and someone else's by mistake. I have been as much as 70 pounds overweight and if you are only 5 foot 3 inches tall, like me, that's FAT!

Whether you look obese or thin, you can still be physically unfit. I learned about physical fitness when I went into the Army. I was nineteen years old and had a body that would start a war, like the one fought over Helen of Troy, yet I could not walk up two flights of stairs without being out of breath and my upper body strength was almost non-existent. Once I joined the Army, we had physical training five days a week. I could barely run a half-mile, I could do about 10 sit-ups, and push-ups were flat out of the question. However, after a few weeks I was able to run two miles in less than 20 minutes, I could do about 50 sit-ups, and I could do 20 good push-ups. I never knew how unfit I was until my body was put through a fitness test.

Today, I am glad I had that experience because, those moments in time, prepared me for my constant "battle of the bulge." For me, working to remain physically fit is the area where I need the most discipline. There are others who have a similar need. Even though I knew what to do, I still would not do it. I was not taking care of the one thing that housed my soul and my mind, and provided me with the strength to achieve my goals…my body! I am writing about what has worked for me. Throughout this action guide, I have written about true situations that either others or I have gone through. This chapter will be no different. I would like to start by reminding each of you that visualization plays a very important role in physical fitness and weight loss. That is why it is so important to complete each task in this exercise.

Exercising regularly will become a part of your daily regiment, if you develop the habit of doing it on a regular basis. It can lower your cholesterol level and reduce your chances of heart disease, control anxiety, depression, and obesity. Becoming physically fit can also help you think clearer and increase your self-esteem.

If you are not exercising regularly, it is probably because you have convinced yourself that you do not have time. Could it possibly be that you do not make time because you do not like exercising. The best way to minimize your dislike for exercising is to find a series of exercises that are fun and do them with a friend or group of friends. It is also helpful if you come up with a set time to exercise and write it down each time you work out. If you have no idea of the kind of physical fitness regiment you want to implement, you may want to begin by visiting your nearest fitness center for ideas or look into getting a fitness trainer. Below are listed some fitness programs you may want to consider:

Power Walking	Dancing
Treadmill	Aerobics
Swimming	Skiing
Tennis	Softball (regularly)
Martial Arts Classes	Weightlifting

Join Fitness Spa   Biking
Badminton   Racquetball
Ballroom Dancing   Volleyball
Basketball   Golf
Roller Skating

Very Important Note: Please make sure you visit your doctor before attempting any fitness program or diet.

You should choose more than one type of fitness program and alternate. That will prevent boredom and the variety should take away the feeling that you have to do tedious exercises.

If you decide that you would like to begin by exercising at home by viewing Digital videos (DVDs), you may want to purchase your own DVDs and start a collection. Browse through the physical fitness section and choose at least three DVDs that will give you a full body workout. For areas such as the hips, stomach, and thighs, you may need to spend extra time exercising these areas, if they are problem areas for you, but make sure you do your full body workout first and do not over exert yourself or overwork your muscles.

Exercise: Using a calendar, mark the day you will begin your exercise program. Mark the number of days you intend to exercise weekly. (I recommend that you exercise no less than three days a week.) Next, write down the types of fitness programs you will be using for the next month. Then, make a commitment out loud everyday, that you are going to follow your fitness program until you reach your desired goal. If you continue on your program without failing, you should notice a change in your physical appearance within 6 to 8 weeks. How quickly your physique changes will depend on your eating habits and your metabolism.

Remember: Please make sure you visit your doctor before attempting any fitness program or diet.

Power Tip: In addition to verbalizing your commitment to become physically fit, spend some time visualizing it also. See yourself having the kind of body you would like to have and see it in your mind everyday. Remember, if you want to achieve excellence, the mind, body, and soul must work together. If you need help staying inspired, visit the healthy and happy section at www.designingyourlifetoday.com.

Don't Quit!

When things go wrong, as they sometimes will
When the road you're trudging seems all up hill
When funds are low and the debts are high
And you want to smile, but you have to sigh
When care is pressing you down a bit
Rest, if you must, but don't you quit
Life is queer with its twists and turns
As every one of us sometimes learns
And many a failure turns about
When he might have won had he stuck it out
Don't give up, though the pace seems slow
You may succeed with another blow
Success is failure turned inside out
The silver tint of the clouds of doubt
And you never can tell how close you are
It may be near when it seems so far
So stick to the fight when you're hardest hit
It's when things seem worst that you must not quit.
--Author Unknown

Let's Eat!

Dieting is no fun, so do not do it, unless, your physician recommends it. If you want to become physically fit, you have to eat healthy. That does not mean you starve yourself. Much of what you have learned throughout this workbook has to do with state of mind, because the mind, body, and soul must work together, you will have to rely on your mind (visualization) and not your feelings to bring the body along.

Exercise: This exercise has many parts, so take the time to thoroughly complete each one. We have numbered each exercise for your convenience.

I. Begin by using visualizations and affirmations. Affirm out loud that you are going to be healthy. Say it now! "I am going to be healthy"! Say it again! Now, say it again, but say it until you feel the commitment you are making to yourself. Feel the passion behind your words. Do not go to the next exercise until you feel the passion and sincerity behind your words.

II. Using the power of your imagination, visualize yourself as you would like to be. Do this no less than three times a day. If you have a picture of the way you want to look, have it in front of you when you are visualizing your new body. Note:

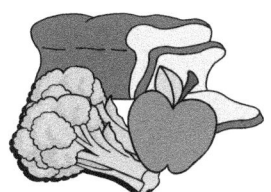 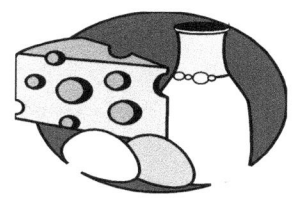

Do exercises I & II everyday, until you reach your goal.

III. Nothing ever gets accomplished without order, so this exercise involves you organizing your kitchen and writing out your menus for the next 14 days. After completing your menus for the next 14 days, continue at the end of the first seven days to write out 7-day menus. Do this at the end of each week until this becomes a normal part of your daily routine. All menus should consist of low fat, high nutritious and energizing foods. If you have no idea how to get started, contact your physician, visit your local library, or you may use some of the recipe books listed below. Most of them have full menus pre-arranged for you.

The menu used by the author has been published for your convenience. This menu was used for the first 90 days, only. You may use it as a guide for establishing your menu.

You may consider using some of the books listed below, when writing out your menu:

Weight Watchers, 365-Day Menu Cookbook
Joan Lunden's, Healthy Cooking
Weight Watchers, Cut The Fat Cookbook
Betty Crocker's, New Choice Cookbook

Listed below is a copy of the menu the author used for the first 90 days of her fitness program:

On **Monday**, **Wednesday**, and **Friday** eat the following:

Breakfast	-	4 Egg Whites, ½ Bagel, 1 cup of strawberries
Snack	-	Grapes, Cantaloupe, 1Apple and peanut butter
Lunch	-	Tuna or Chicken Breast (6oz.), Steamed Broccoli, ½ Cup Rice
Snack	-	Low Calorie Protein Shake
Dinner	-	Baked Chicken, Vegetables, ½ Baked Potato

On **Tuesday**, **Thursday**, **Saturday**, and **Sunday** eat the following:

Breakfast	-	1 Cup Oatmeal, 1 Cup Applesauce
Snack	-	Low Calorie Protein Shake
Lunch	-	Whole Wheat Turkey Sandwich w/mustard
Snack	-	Yogurt
Dinner	-	3oz. Baked Salmon, ½ Cup Steamed Asparagus, ½ Whole Wheat Bread

Of course, the key is to plan your menus so that you will have a variety of meals. That will help you stick with a healthy eating plan.

HEALTH

It doesn't matter if you have all the wealth,
Your life is nothing without your health.
So use discretion in all you eat,
Chew vegetables, fruits, and lean meats.

Write your commitment to become healthy below:

THE JOY OF LIFE
(Learn To Be)

In this day and time we want everything right away and done the way we want it done. No one wants to wait for the "gold" or best outcome. We want to make the gold ourselves and give it our own value. Well, there is a time to put a value on things in life and there is a time to put the value on ourselves and let life put the value on what we are to receive. In other words, there are parts of life that cannot be controlled, should not be controlled, and parts that we would not want to control, if we are going to get the best outcome. Sometimes it is wiser to simply let things "BE" and that includes learning to be. If you are a "control freak," it may be time for you to relax and allow a part of your life to run its natural course. Everything is not meant to be controlled. If you learn to let go you may find that you will obtain more good things out of life than you ever expected. Here are some of the reasons why it is important to learn to "BE."

1. **It can decrease misery** - If you really want joy, learn to accept parts of life you cannot control or change. Trust that God will change them for the better or bring the outcome you want. You will definitely become a much happier individual. Not only will you be happy, others who have to deal with you will find it more pleasurable to be around you.

2. **It will increase your trust** - It is okay to desire a particular outcome to a certain situation concerning your life: however, it is more important to release your attachment to the outcome. By releasing your attachment to the outcome of certain situations, you are showing that you have confidence in yourself and that you trust that God's will, for your life will only bring you the best.

3. You will achieve inner peace – Some have laughed and underrated the idea of achieving inner peace. If that is the case with you that only means you have not learned to "BE." Once you have achieved inner peace you will discover a new light in your life. You will learn to walk without fear, you will discover your purpose in life and your light will touch someone else's life.

Learning to "BE" means you will move the person you think you are "out of the way" and become the person you are meant to be. That will allow you to contribute to the greater good for your life and for mankind. If you have little or no joy in your life, it is because you have not learned to release your control over yourself and others (not to be confused with discipline). The more controlling you are the more you block joy and other good things you are supposed to receive. You even block the flow of true love and the wealth of life that is rightfully yours. Whatever is meant for you cannot be taken away by others; however, by not releasing control, you can inadvertently give away your own treasures. If you have a hard time learning to "BE," practice meditating on a Biblical scripture or meditating by clearing your mind and the peace you need in order to "BE" still will come. Commit to doing this today, because there is always "power in the present moment."

How to Meditate

It is not always easy to sit still and let the right things come to you. Especially if it is something you have been hoping for over a long period of time. We sometimes feel as though we have to make things happen. That may be the time to let go and allow something to happen. When waiting seems difficult, learning to be still through meditation can help. Meditating is more important to your personal happiness and personal growth than you may know. Meditation can aid in clearing the mind, making it easier to attract the things that are desired. Meditation can help clear an emotional path and we can receive what we are meant to have. Meditation also helps to increase discipline, helping us to consistently take action and achieve goals and to follow through with a true purpose in life. Meditation can also lower blood pressure, anxiety and stress levels.

Spending some quiet time with yourself can help you sort out the details of any problem and possibly receive solutions. Through prayer and proper meditation, you can truly learn more about the essence of who you are. One of the most important aspects of meditation is that during your quiet time you can hear from God. That is why praying and meditation should be done together. If praying is talking to God, we can safely assume that meditating is listening to God. It is very difficult to hear from God if you are always surrounded by noise or if you are always doing the talking through prayer. There are times to be still. Take some time and read about the various heroes and heroines of the Bible. They all meditated at some point and once they were able to hear God and they obeyed his words, they received their greatest rewards. People often talk about how busy they are.

How can anyone be too busy to take the time to do what it takes to have a better life?

There are many levels of meditation, but for the purposes of this book, I will give a beginners' version. If you are not accustomed to meditating, the first time you try to sit quietly with yourself may not be easy. You may hear all kinds of thoughts going through your mind or you may hear one sound after another constantly interrupting your thoughts. If that keeps happening to you, you will need to create your own sounds to block out all the unnecessary thoughts and sounds. This is called a *Mantra (Mahn-tra)*. I usually sound out the word *"God," (G-ah – ah-a – h –d)* over and over, until my mind becomes quiet. You may use the *"God"* or the word *"ah."* I feel a greater sense of peace when I use the word *"God."* Another way to quiet your mind would be to listen to music designed to help you meditate. You can find some online or in most department stores. It will be labeled as meditation music. You can also visit, www.shop.designingyourlifetoday.com for suitable music to download.

Follow the instructions below to go through the meditation process:

1. Make sure you are positioned comfortably. You may sit or lay down.

2. Take a deep breath in and begin chanting your mantra as you breathe out. If you have decided to use music simply breathe in using 4 or 5 counts and breathe out using 4 or 5 counts.

3. Repeat the process at least three (3) times. Remember, not to breathe in and out too fast, you don't want to make yourself dizzy. Breathe in and out slowly.

4. Continue to breathe in and out slowly, but you should be able to stop repeating your mantra and start visualizing.

5. Visualize something that you want to receive or in your mind ask for the solution to a problem you have been trying to solve. Sometimes you may want to clear you mind and just be.

6. Be aware of any visions or words that pop into your mind. These may be the solutions you have been searching for.

7. Remember to visualize what you want. For example: If you want love or a mate visualize the kind of mate you want. Visualize the characteristics you want in a mate and not a particular person. True love is not about physical features. If you want wealth, visualize the things you intend to buy with the money.

CAUTION: Meditation does work if done properly. Be careful not to visualize or wish for something bad or unpleasant to happen to someone else. That will backfire! You will begin to attract unpleasant things into your own life.

Power Tip: Remember, if you choose to sound out a mantra, make sure the sound comes from the center of your body. Your diaphragm should relax and vibrate with sound.

Use the space below to write down your meditative thoughts:

Happiness at a Glance

Here are a few last minute tips to help you express happiness and keep you feeling good:

1. SMILE
2. Say "hello" to someone
3. Compliment others
4. Give whenever possible
5. Plan an exciting trip
6. Take up a new hobby
7. Learn something you have always wanted to learn
8. Dedicate a day to yourself
9. Don't hold onto negative energy
10. Listen to upbeat, happy music
11. Stay away from negative people
12. Work at becoming physically fit
13. Eat healthy and exercise
14. Release your attachment to things
15. Release your attachment to outcomes
16. Trust God
17. Learn to be yourself
18. Always feed your self-esteem
19. Learn to tame your ego
20. Be childlike and have fun
21. Take a nice, hot bubble bath
22. Don't take yourself or life too seriously
23. Buy a pet
24. Make a new friend
25. Help someone
26. Hug someone
27. Laugh, just laugh
28. Be still
29. Really stop and smell the flowers
30. Love, Love, Love

What to Do With Your New Information

Congratulations on completing volume I of your quest for success. If you did not complete every exercise, I urge you to go back and do so. If you did complete all the exercises, you are now feeling more confident and ready to experience life as the new you. The information you now have was designed to show you that you have the ability to live the kind of life you have been dreaming of. Because the journey to success, fulfillment, and self-actualization is an ongoing one, **High Impact Power Principles, Volume II** will deal with more step by step information for going to the next level and it will deal with specifics of how to manifest your desires while establishing a strong values system. Growth is done one step at a time. Now that you have established clear goals and uncovered vital information concerning yourself, you are ready to handle situations in a more positive manner. Listed below are some final suggestions. These suggestions will help you continue getting the maximum benefits from the exercises you have completed in this workbook.

Some suggestions for maximum benefits are:

- Place your "I Am" list on your refrigerator where you can read them everyday. You will be going to the refrigerator often for water (assuming you drink water cold), because of the recommendation, in this workbook to drink lots of water in the Body section. If not, you will be going for food of some type.

- Take a copy of your goals and shrink them down to purse or wallet size. If you do not have access to a copier, visit your nearest copy center or office supply store and have a copy made (there is a small fee involved). Carry these goals and read them no less than three times everyday.

- Once you have discovered your "True Purpose" spend some time seeking additional information by reading or interviewing others who are in your area of interest.

- After completing your dream sheet, pick at least one dream and commit to bringing it into reality. Once you have achieved that goal, pick another, and so on.

- If you miss a deadline date on your plan of action sheet, re-dedicate yourself to achieving the goal, set a new date and get back to work.

- After listening to the recommended CDs and MP3s, share what you have learned with a friend. This will help you remember what you have heard. Invite your friend to purchase a copy. Please do not give them the material, it is copyrighted and you want them to invest in their self the same way you invested in yourself. It will inspire them to release their power. Remember we reap what we sow and if we sow dishonesty, do not expect a positive return.

- Make sure you place your commitment board where you can see it. Pay attention to it, daily. You may add new pictures whenever you like.

- Meditate and visualize your goals and dreams everyday.

- As you come up with new goals, write them on your goal sheet. You do not have to accomplish everything right away.

- Feel free to have fun with a friend when doing the "One Fine Day" exercise.

Remember: If you skipped any exercises, please go back and complete them.

Record Your Power Thoughts Below:

"Remember, parents are nothing more than human beings who earned the title because of your birth. They can be wrong and they make mistakes. Give them a break and yourself, too. As an adult, you are responsible for releasing the best energy and using your personal power to achieve. If you decide not to use it, it is not your parents' or anybody else's fault. Your success in life is totally up to you. Go for it, because I believe you have the power to excel."

Pat A. Council

ABOUT PAT COUNCIL

Pat Council is an empowerment specialist, success consultant, and writer who specializes in helping others recognize and release their success potential. Pat is the CEO of True Thoroughbred Enterprises, Inc., a personal development company. As the owner of True Thoroughbred Enterprises, Inc., Pat uses her areas of expertise to help individuals and small business owners improve their daily performance, so they will achieve their desired income. Pat has study courses that aids people with getting in touch with their authentic self, gaining clarity on goals, and courses that guide others toward taking results-oriented action. Her goal is to inspire and enlighten others to courageously be their best. Pat is an author, radio show host, speaker, and a master sales trainer.

The effectiveness of Pat's teachings is proven by the daily growing audience of thousands that listen to her online radio show, **"Designing Your Life, Today." (Visit: www.designingyourlifetoday.com for more information.)** Pat has created systems that allow even the busiest person to learn techniques and practical methods for tapping into their potential and releasing their power to succeed at their highest level. As a speaker Pat delivers words with power that inspires others to become independent thinkers and take action. Her goal is to help others become an asset to themselves and to any organization they are connected to. Being a fan of creative self-expression, Pat writes, sings, dances, and gives enlightening, entertaining speeches.

Pat Council is the author of the self-help book, "**High Impact Power Principles, Volume I**" and the creator of "**Let's Get H.I.P.P.**" (pronounced Hip), a high energy self-improvement seminar, which also has been tailored into an inspiring speech.

She has also created other empowering programs on CD or MP3 Downloads such as "**7 Ways to Create the Flow of Money**", "**5 Power Tips for Direct Sales Success**", and "**Success is Now**". Her newest book, **P.O.W.E.R.** will be released soon, along with **"The P.O.W.E.R"** Training Program designed for almost any organization or corporation. Pat delivers top notch training to those on the journey to success through webinars. (**Visit: patcouncil.com for more information**).

Life Before the Radio Show, Speaking, and Writing Pat served as a soldier in the United States Army. She is a former salesperson who has won more than 50 awards in the area of real estate. As a realtor she sold over $40,000,000 worth of real estate. She earned numerous awards as a member of a fortune 500 cosmetics company where she ranked in the top 2% in a sales force of more than 1 million cosmetic distributors. Pat is proficient in real estate investing, small business coaching and an expert at sales training. She has helped many new and experienced sales people, as well as small business owners, produce higher incomes and reach their sales goals. She has also lead several sales teams to the winner's circle. Pat is also a graduate of the University of Maryland, and she has studied in the areas of marketing, law, and journalism at the University of North Florida. She is also a talented singer. Pat owned a successful real estate company until she decided to devote her daily work toward helping others become more successful by releasing their potential by using their God-given talents and by providing personal empowerment information on her radio show, "Designing Your Life, Today" She believes that all people should live the life they deserve provided they are willing to take action and responsibility for their own success. Pat has been a successful entrepreneur since 1989.

To hire Pat as a speaker or to receive more information call 904-519-5443 or send an email to:
patcouncil@patcouncil.com

Want to tap into your power, release your potential to serve your purpose and live a passionate life?

Tune into Pat Council's online radio show:
"Designing Your Life Today"

Visit the website for free Success Tips and more information

www.designingyourlifetoday.com

View our line of "Power Source" Products at:

www.shop.designingyourlifetoday.com

-Receive answers to questions you have about success and achievement!

-Get more information about Pat Council, by visiting:
www.patcouncil.com

-View a list of seminars and speeches offered at
www.patcouncil.com

E-mail or write us with questions to:

E-mail: info@designingyourlifetoday.com or patcouncil@patcouncil.com

True Thoroughbred Enterprises, Inc.
Attn: Pat Council
9930 Chelsea Lake Road
Jacksonville, Fl 32256
904-519-5443

Why You Should Buy This Book?

"It's hard to be around Pat and not be affected by her. Her book High Impact Power Principles will definitely have a positive effect on you! Looking to make a change? This book is for you."

Tommy Ford, Actor
"As seen on New York Undercover"

❖❖❖❖

"Pat's, High Impact Power Principles, Action Guide is properly named. This Action Guide will definitely put you back on the right track or jump start your life and take you into high gear! You'll be glad you bought this book."

Willie Jolley
Speaker and Best Selling
Author of "The Motivational Minute"

❖❖❖❖

"Pat Council is a leader and a success story. Pat's willingness to share the bounty God has given her is not only important, but admirable. This workbook is an extension of Pat's seminar and a labor of love. It represents a deep commitment to provide its reader and user a road map to success. If one is smart enough to acquire it and use it, I promise all that is due you will come to you. Thank you Pat for sharing with us the light from your candle."

George C. Fraser
Author, "Race for Success" and
"Success Runs In Our Race"

❖❖❖❖

This book will help you identify some of your obstacles to success, and it can help you overcome them. It is also good to use before you get started on your journey toward winning or fulfillment of your purpose. Take the time to get a grip on things and learn to live your life to the fullest!

ISBN 0-9716919-0-8

www.ingramcontent.com/pod-product-compliance
Lightning Source LLC
LaVergne TN
LVHW081357060426
835510LV00016B/1874